The Care and Training of

Home Cage Birds

BY BERNARD POE

Copyright © 2013 Read Books Ltd.
This book is copyright and may not be
reproduced or copied in any way without
the express permission of the publisher in writing

British Library Cataloguing-in-Publication Data
A catalogue record for this book is available from the
British Library

Aviculture

'Aviculture' is the practice of keeping and breeding birds, as well as the culture that forms around it, and there are various reasons why people get involved in Aviculture. Some people breed birds to preserve a specific species, usually due to habitat destruction, and some people breed birds (especially parrots) as companions, and yet others do this to make a profit. Aviculture encourages conservation, provides education about avian species, provides companion birds for the public, and includes research on avian behaviour. It is thus a highly important and enjoyable past time. There are avicultural societies throughout the world, but generally in Europe, Australia and the United States, where people tend to be more prosperous, having more leisure time to invest. The first avicultural society in Australia was The Avicultural Society of South Australia, founded in 1928. It is now promoted with the name Bird Keeping in Australia. The two major national avicultural societies in the United States are the American Federation of Aviculture and the Avicultural Society of America, founded in 1927. In the UK, the Avicultural Society was formed in 1894 and the Foreign Bird League in 1932. The Budgerigar Society was formed in 1925.

Some of the most popular domestically kept birds are finches and canaries. 'Finches' are actually a broader category, encompassing canaries, and make fantastic domestic birds, capable of living long and healthy lives if given the requisite care. Most species are very easy to breed, and usefully do not grow too large (unlike their larger compatriot the budgerigar), and so do not need a massive living space. 'Canary' (associated with the *Serinus canaria*), is a song bird is native to the Canary Islands, Madeira, and the Azores – and has long been kept as a cage bird in Europe, beginning in the 1470s. It now enjoys an international following, and the terms *canariculture* and *canaricultura* have been used in French, Spanish and Italian respectively, to describe the keeping and breeding of canaries. It is only gradually however (a testament to its growing popularity) that English breeders are beginning to use such terms. Canaries are now the most popular form of finch kept in Britain and are often found still fulfilling their historic role of protecting underground miners. Canaries like budgies, are seed eaters, which need to dehusk the seed before feeding on the kernel. However, unlike budgerigars, canaries are perchers. The average life span of a canary is five years, although they have been known to live twice as long.

Parakeets or 'Budgies' (a type of parrot) are another incredibly popular breed of domestic bird, and are originally from Australia, first brought to Europe in the 1840s. Whilst they are naturally green with yellow heads and black bars on the wings in the wild, domesticated budgies come in a massive variety of colours. They have the toes and beak typical of parrot like birds, as in nature they are climbers; budgies are hardy seed eaters and their strong beak is utilised for dehusking seeds as well as a climbing aid. When kept indoors however, it is important to supplement their diet of seeds with fresh fruit and vegetables, which would be found in the wild. Budgies are social birds, so it is most important to make sure they have company, preferably of their own kind. They do enjoy human companionship though, and may be persuaded, if gently stroked on the chest feathers to perch on one's finger. If not kept in an aviary, they need a daily period of free flight, but great care must be taken not to let them escape.

Last, but most definitely not least, perhaps the most popular breed of domestic bird, is the 'companion parrot' – a general term used for *any* parrot kept as a pet that interacts with its human counterpart. Generally, most species of parrot can make good companions. Common domestic parrots include large birds such as Amazons, African Greys, Cockatoos, Eclectus, Hawk-headed Parrots and Macaws; mid-sized birds such as Caiques, Conures, Quakers, Pionus, Poicephalus, Rose-Ringed parakeets and Rosellas, and many of the smaller types including Budgies, Cockatiels, Parakeets, lovebirds, Parrotlets and Lineolated Parakeets. The *Convention on International Trade in Endangered Species of Wild Fauna and Flora* (also known as CITES) has made the trapping and trade of all wild parrots illegal, because taking parrots from the wild has endangered or reduced some of the rarer or more valuable species. However, many parrot species are still common; and some abundant parrot species may still be legally killed as crop pests in their native countries. Endangered parrot species are better suited to conservation breeding programs than as companions.

Parrots can be very rewarding pets to the right owners, due to their intelligence and desire to interact with people. Many parrots are very affectionate, even cuddly with trusted people, and require a lot of attention from their owners. Some species have a tendency to bond to one or two people, and dislike strangers, unless they are regularly and consistently handled by different people. Properly socialized parrots can be friendly, outgoing and confident companions. Most pet parrots take readily to trick training as well, which can help deflect their energy and correct many behavioural problems. Some owners successfully use well behaved parrots as therapy animals. In fact, many have even trained their parrots to wear parrot harnesses (most easily accomplished with young birds) so that they can be taken to enjoy themselves outdoors in a relatively safe manner without the risk of flying away. Parrots are prey animals and even the tamest pet may fly off if spooked. Given the right care and attention, keeping birds is usually problem free. It is hoped that the reader enjoys this book.

Contents

Introduction	1
When You Buy a Bird	6
The Cage, Its Furnishings and Care	11
Ten Rules for Maintaining Your Bird in Good Health	17
Common Cage Bird Ailments and Their Treatments	19
Treatment of Birds During the Molting Period	41
How to Tell the Sex and Age of Cage Birds	44
The Length of Life of Cage Birds	46
The Mating and Breeding of Cage Birds	48
Some Good Cage-Bird Foods	53
Native Wild Plants as Sources of Cage-Bird Foods	57
When You Buy a Parrot	61
Care of Parrots	65
Feeding Parakeets	71
Psittacosis or Parrot Fever	73
The Reproductive Systems of the Cock and Hen	75
The Digestive System of Birds	79
The Respiratory System of Birds	83
The Circulatory System of Birds	86
A Word About Out-of-Door Aviaries	89
The Training of Cage Birds	96
12 Bird Plates	99
Bibliography	111
Index	115

Introduction

Canaries

Cage birds have been under domestication since the very earliest times. The most popular of these small songbirds used as pets have always been the members of the great finch, or *Fringillidae* family, and especially the canaries.

The domestication of canaries as cage birds is as obscure in origin as is that of most of our other numerous domestic creatures, whether animal or plant. It seems probable that the first canaries were captured for use as cage birds in the Canary Islands. These were first described scientifically, and named, by Linnaeus with his system of nomenclature, as set forth in his *Systema Naturae*, first published in 1735. The name given these birds by the famous founder of our biological nomenclature was *Serinus serinus canarius*. There is another bird which might equally have been the source of our present-day canaries, a bird known as the Serin Finch, also first described by Linnaeus and known as *Serinus serinus serinus*. The repetition of these names, and the whole subject of the rules of biological nomenclature is too elaborate to be gone into here, but it now rests upon a more certain foundation than ever before in the history of science. The Serin Finch is found throughout southern Europe. Both in central and southern Europe, and in the Canary Islands, bird catching and caging and breeding were established among the nobility and gentry very early in history; the custom spread rapidly thereafter throughout the civilized world. Probably both the Serin Finches and the canaries were established there for many years.

These two birds are, in their wild state, so closely similar as to be distinguished with certainty only by students of ornithology. They both show upper parts of gray, tinged with olive green, especially on the rump, the feathers usually possessing darker shafts. The under parts are a clear pure yellow, or a sulphur color, and the flanks and sides are streaked with gray. The feet and legs are yellowish brown; the upper mandible, or beak, is dark brown throughout almost all its length; the lower mandible is a pale yellow or yellowish brown. The Wild Canary *(Serinus serinus canarius)* is grayer above than the Serin Finch, and shows less yellowish and greenish; the rump is a duller dingier yellow, and the bill is somewhat larger. Sometimes this increase in size is very pronounced; but usually the difference is slight.

The true Wild Canary *(Serinus serinus canarius)* inhabits the Canary Islands, except the islands of Lanzarote and Fuerteventura. It is also found on the Azores and Madeira.

The Serin Finch *(Serinus serinus serinus)* is found in southern Europe, northern Africa, Palestine, and Asia Minor. The habitats of both birds are similar—open country where small trees and bushes abound; in thickets, vineyards, and similar places. Their food consists partly of figs and other small fruits, but chiefly of small seeds of all kinds. Their nests are small neat cups artfully woven together and composed externally of small pliant weed stems, weed bark, and grasses. On the inside they are lined with soft plant down and hair and fine, soft grasses. They are placed in the lower branches of small twiggy trees and bushes, or sometimes in tangles of vines. The eggs are green,

INTRODUCTION

spotted and blotched with deep magenta, violet, and brown, and the number in a normal clutch varies from three to five. Two broods are ordinarily raised each year, in early spring, and in midsummer.

The first records of canaries as cage birds seems to be toward the end of the sixteenth century, in Italy, whence the birds had come by way of the Canary Islands and the Island of Elba. They soon appeared in Germany and in England; in these countries especially they have been developed to a high degree of domesticity and selective breeding. The British have been the greatest breeders of canaries in the world; their birds are bred chiefly for color and plumage and form of body. The National Exhibition for canary breeders is a very large and very important annual affair. In December of 1948 some 5,400 birds were exhibited in a great showing held in the historic Crystal Palace. Hundreds of canary societies and clubs have sprung up all over the United Kingdom, and fancy-bird breeding has assumed proportions there unknown elsewhere. The German fanciers breed chiefly for song; the famous Roller Canary is their especial contribution. They also are the greatest commercial handlers of canaries and cage birds in the world.

Other Small Cage Birds

Whatever is said about canaries applies equally to the other members of the finch family. The most popular finches other than canaries, in this country at least, are the Society Finches, Strawberry Finch, Masked Grass Finch, Shaft-Tailed Finch, Saffron Finch, Spice Finch, Lady Gould Finch, Butterfly Finch, Zebra Finch, the Fire Finches, the Waxbills, European Goldfinch, Bullfinch, Ribbon Finch, Silverbill, the Cardinals.

Other birds also popular as cage birds, though not

nearly so common as the canaries, are the Weaverbirds and the Whydas. These are closely related in habits and food requirements to the finches.

Still other small cage birds, known as the soft-billed birds (because their bills are less adapted to the cracking of seeds than to the feeding upon insects and small fruits, and small invertebrates such as spiders, slugs, worms, and the like), are sometimes offered for sale in the pet stores. These rather unusual birds demand food and care somewhat different from the canaries. If you desire to keep such birds, first consult the Bibliography, on pages 111-114 and select a guide which will assist you in their special care. Some of these uncommon cage birds are the Tanagers, the Troupial or Bugle Bird, the Pekin Nightingale, often also called the Chinese Nightingale, Japanese Nightingale or Japanese Robin *(Leiothrix luteus)*, the Shama Thrush, the Yellow-winged Sugarbird, and the amusing Jay Thrushes.

Birds other than canaries form only about twenty-five per cent of the birds popularly kept as home cage birds. These include the psittacine birds, that is, Parrots, Parakeets, Lovebirds, Macaws, Cockatiels, Conures, and so on.

The members of this group are larger birds and, to some people, more attractive songbirds. However, it can be said that no other birds have become so thoroughly domesticated, so tame, and so much attached to their owners; certainly, no other of our pet birds are so long-lived. They are usually very brilliantly colored birds as well, and their antics are highly amusing. One must consider, however, that they are subject to the disease known as psitticosis, which is serious and easily transmissible to humans. They are apt to be vicious, and usually will injure smaller birds if put into the same cage with them. In addition their voices are not particularly pleasant, and many of them give

INTRODUCTION

vent to harsh screams, and other loud raucous noises, which, however, can be quickly silenced by a thick cloth thrown over the cage.

In spite of these drawbacks, which are not present in the case of the smaller songbirds, many people become very fond of their psittacine pets, and their keep and breeding forms a large part of the hobby of bird raising and home-pet keeping.

The most popular members of this group are the delicately colored little parakeets, sometimes known as Lovebirds, but also as Shell Parakeets, Budgerygahs, Grass Parakeets, and Undulated Grass Parakeets.

Like the canaries, members of the parrot family have been under domestication from very early times. There is a record, for example, of the parrot, which is said to have spoken fluent Senegalese and French, and which was presented to Queen Marie Antoinette about 1780 by the Chevalier de Bouffleurs, Governor of Senegal.

Suggestions for the home-keeping of the smaller cage birds will be found beginning on page 11; and for the keeping of the various members of the parrot tribe, beginning on page 65.

When You Buy a Bird

When you purchase a bird, be sure that you know accurately its sex (see page 44). Make certain that it is in good physical condition, and that it is a young bird, not an old one whose powers are already on the wane. Read over the paragraphs on pages 44 and 45 and familiarize yourself with the various points of bird anatomy that you should consider. Of course, you do not need to depend on your own knowledge completely, for any reputable bird dealer will sell you just the kind of a bird you desire, and in most cases you can safely trust his judgement. However, it is interesting to know about these things for yourself. If you are purchasing a singing bird you will naturally ask to hear it sing before you make your purchase. Even if you are buying a bird chiefly for its cheerful actions and bright colors, it is well also to get one that can sing into the bargain. It is most pleasant in the morning after you have risen for the day to be greeted with a bright song, and especially cheering, when you return from your work at the end of the day to be similarly welcomed.

Here a word of caution must be given; do not purchase a bird whose song is too loud, shrill and high-pitched. Sometimes, in a bird store, with other noises going on, either inside or outside, or both, a bird's song may sound just right; but in the quiet of your home you may find that the song is altogether too loud. Moreover, a loud, shrill, piercing birdsong in the home is not at all to be desired! Such sounds assailing the ear day after day produce nervousness and irritability in the hearers before they are aware of what is causing the condition. Quiet, soft, melodious, leisurely songs are what one should listen for in purchasing a bird. So decide on what sort of a bird you want, before going out to look for one. Don't let any dealer talk you into buying this bird or that; don't let him make up your mind for you. His taste in bird music or color may be very different from yours. Remember that some birds are purchased for their bright colors; some for their interesting, quiet, petlike habits; some for their vocal powers. Others, like the mynahs, are bought for their imitative, amusing notes; others like the parrots and budgerygahs for their talking powers.

After you have bought your bird and brought it home, and perhaps put it into its new cage, stay away from it for a few hours or a day, so that it may have plenty of time to become accustomed to its new quarters and have leisure to investigate every nook and corner of its new abode. Then approach it gradually. A great deal of harm may be done to a new bird's nervous system by subjecting it at once to bustling scrutiny, loud conversational tones, quick nervous actions, attempts to feed it or talk to it or amuse it. Let it alone for half a day at the least. Let it quiet down naturally. Then slowly approach the cage, talking to the bird in a soft, high-pitched voice, a little sort of bird voice, as it were. Remember that small birds do not hear the lower and perhaps not even the middle tones of the human voice, especially of the voices of men. The rule would seem to be: when in the presence of a canary, talk in canary tones, but when in the presence of a duck, talk in low-pitched duck tones.

In offering your new friend food and water, let

your offering movements be very slow and deliberate; make no quick jerky, nervous movements.

Speak to your bird as you feed or water it in gentle soothing tones. Like Bottom, "speak in a monstrous little voice." When you give your bird food, you might try the experiment of saying "FOOD," in a deep low tone; then try pursing your lips up and saying "weee" in a high thin voice; or purse your lips up and make little kissing and squeaking noises, and see how your bird chirks up at once. Take immediate notice of these sounds. Thus you will learn at the outset in just what tone and pitch of voice to talk to your bird. It is the next best thing to learning the language of birds; perhaps it is the language of birds, for all their squeakings, chippings, hissings, chirpings, cooings, and songnotes are what constitute the vocabulary of their speech. Thus after a time you will be talking to your bird, and he, perchance, will be answering you after his fashion, to his evident interest and pleasure.

Be careful lest your children (or perhaps some of your callers) frighten your bird; let all motions around its cage be slow and gentle. Especially caution your maid not to flourish a dust cloth too violently near the cage. A large waving piece of cloth will frighten a bird perhaps more than anything else. Possibly it arouses in the dim consciousness of the bird a vague memory of the time when in its remote ancestry it had to dodge the flapping and swooping of a hawk or other predatory creature.

One of the very best ways to make friends with a new bird is to put a little soft bird food, or some small seeds on the tip of your finger, which has been previously moistened with a drop of honey. Rub these, so they will adhere, onto the bars of the cage. If your motions are deliberate, the bird will invariably take an immediate interest in what is going on, and will

WHEN YOU BUY A BIRD

soon hop over to investigate, and will begin, after a short scrutiny, to pick at the seeds. Soon he will be taking these from the tip of your finger and, later perhaps, from between your lips—if you like that sort of thing!

If you wish to train your bird to sit on your finger or to be taken out of his cage on your hand, wait for his first training period until near nightfall when he is about to settle down on his perch to roost. (One of my little friends when she saw this roosting process going on, said, "Well, that's the first time I ever saw a bird in bed.") When your bird is beginning to settle down for the night, open the cage door gradually and put your finger in parallel with the perch. Then gently slide the perch away, substituting your finger for it, and your bird will eventually shift over by little and little onto your finger. Hold your finger still a moment until he has his little toes firmly clasped over it, and then very gradually indeed withdraw him from the cage.

This takes a good deal of practice, and you may have to work at this a long time before he begins to feel quite safe and secure on your finger, and stops trying to get back into the cage every time he gets as far as the door. Very soon he will be leaving your finger and hopping up onto your arm or shoulder, or where not! If your little friend, astonished at his new liberty, flies off into the room, then is the time for especial calmness on your part. Do not chase him about and make him nervous. Close the windows and doors, and if there is a fireplace, stand in front of it. Let the bird fly about a bit, or perch quietly wherever he wishes. If he is inclined to dash against the window-glass, thinking this offers a free passage to the out-of-doors, move quietly to the window with the cage in your hands, the open door of the cage towards the bird. Usually after a few trials, when the open cage door is within a foot or so of him, he will turn and fly into his familiar barred home. Now let him alone for half an hour or so, if he appears to be highly excited by his novel escapade.

The Cage, Its Furniture and General Care

Home cage birds are not at all unhappy in a cage, for the cage birds we see were all hatched out in a cage and have not known any other life; this is their natural home, their familiar surrounding. Indeed, they would be most unhappy, even terrified, if they were to find themselves outside of a cage, outside of its protecting walls and bars. They would not know how to feed, or where, or on what; they would not know how to bathe, or roost, or nest, or where to find shelter and protection if a cat, or a hawk, or an owl, or a grackle, or any other predator should attack them. So do not feel sorry for a bird in a cage. The condition of affectionate domestication is best for such birds.

Some of the beautiful birds (as for example the lovely little Society Finches) have never existed in a wild state. Nor have their ancestors, since their ancestors were not Society Finches. These birds are purely an artificial crossing, as are others, of canaries, European Goldfinches, and the like. Breeders mate and cross-mate, and by artificial selection have produced, and still are producing, scores of lovely feathered things that have no exact counterparts in wild nature anywhere.

After you have selected your bird, or birds, if you begin with a pair, be sure and get the best advice that the bird dealer can give you. Then, with several good books, you are ready to begin the delight of bird keeping. And first, see to it that your bird has plenty of cage-room. Do not cramp it with too small a cage;

a large cage is essential for the maintenance of the bird's health and spirits. I should suggest a cage that measures at least twenty inches by twelve inches by twelve inches. Some may think this too large, but I should not have it a whit smaller; larger if anything. Remember that even though the bird is confined in a cage, it still likes to use its wings; hence give it plenty of flying space. Flight exercise is very necessary for birds, especially during the molting season.

An all-metal cage is the easiest kind of a cage to keep clean and disinfected, and free from mites and other parasites. The bottom should be of the sliding type, capable of holding sand. Removable containers for food and water are attached to the wires, or made to stand on the bottom of the cage. You can safely trust to your reputable pet store for the proper sort of cages and furniture; there are many kinds.

Around the bottom of the cage and extending up a few inches, place a plastic, or celluloid, or fine-wire-mesh apron. This will prevent seeds and debris being thrown out onto the floor of your room; it will save you a good deal of work. Perches both fixed and swinging may be arranged about the cage. You will be able to exercise a good deal of your own ingenuity on this feature of the cage. But be careful with these perches! Make certain that they are of soft wood—white pine is excellent—for hard harsh perches injure the feet of cage birds, and cause several disorders of the toes, of which we will speak later.

I should advise against a round cage, or a cage with odd angles and tricky corners, or a cage made so as to present a highly ornate appearance; in other words, I advise against any bird fancier trying to see how odd and ornate and unusual a cage he can startle his friends with! The bird's comfort is the first matter to consider: his comfort in plenty of flight room, ease of coming at the food and water dispensers, convenience

THE CAGE, ITS FURNITURE AND GENERAL CARE 13

of the perches, and the like. Keep the bird's comfort in mind also in the matter of the ease with which the cage can be cleaned. A foul cage always results in disease sooner or later. A cage which contains crevices and cracks hard to clean will also usually harbor mites.

Some cages have not only walls of bars, but two or three wooden walls. These wooden, or solid, walls should be painted a soft neutral color; pale green, pale gray, pale blue, pale tan, etc. Use a good hard-drying oil paint, of the glossy sort, which can be most easily washed.

If you must use a second-hand cage or cage furniture see to it that these can be thoroughly cleaned, preferably by long boiling to kill any disease germs that often are present in old equipment. After boiling, disinfect with Lysol, or any good household disinfectant, and again boil for a few minutes to cleanse thoroughly.

Cages may be hung from the ceiling, or from a wall bracket, or supported on a standard after the manner of a floor lamp. The latter support for a cage is the most desirable, for it allows the cage to be placed wherever the owner may wish it.

When you clean the cage, induce the inhabitant to go into a smaller cage—a little wooden one will do nicely, by opening the doors of both cages and putting them together. Put the smaller cage, into which you wish the bird to go, toward the light, as the bird will go much more readily from a dark cage into a light one. It is not necessary to put food or water into the smaller cage, since the bird will be there only during the short time in which his larger home is being cleaned. If he seems restless and flutters about, drape a cloth over the cage, and put it in a nice warm place. The combination of duskiness and warmth will make him comfortably drowsy and contented. It is not recommended to let the bird fly about the room while cleaning the cage—that is, as a regular procedure—for birds that are allowed too much large flying freedom, too often and too regularly, usually lose a good deal of their power of fine song.

Cover the cage at night. Remember that the bird's normal day is from sunrise to sunset. Do not keep your little feathered friend sitting up to all hours of the night under the baleful influence of artificial light.

Keep the cage scrupulously clean; renew the water in the drinking cup every day, and the seeds in the seed cups at least every other day. The sand tray at the bottom of the cage should be removed and cleaned and restored to the cage at least every other day. Wash this tray often, and examine it carefully to detect the presence of worms in the bird's droppings. Watch also for the appearance of mites (see page 38).

Seeds and other foods are often put into cups which are fastened to the sides of the cage; they keep neater and cleaner here than if put onto the bottom of the tray. A piece of cuttlebone should be securely fastened to the wires of the cage, where the birds can readily get at it from a nearby perch. This is not primarily for the purpose of keeping the bird's beak in good condition—though it helps—but is a valuable food adjunct. Never omit it. Cuttlebone (so-called) is a vestigial portion of the skeleton of the squid or cuttlefish and is secreted under the mantle of that creature.

A bird bath is either fastened to the open door of the cage, or else the whole cage stands over it. Whichever type you use must be approved by the bird before he will use it. A new bird may refuse to bathe at first, but will often sit on its perch and fluff and flutter and whirr without going into the water, yet evincing every desire to do so. Let the bird severely alone for a time, with the bath in position, and it will usually go into the water of its own accord, and bathe in its own fashion. If it does not go into the water

THE CAGE, ITS FURNITURE AND GENERAL CARE 15

within twenty minutes' time, remove the bath, for half an hour or so, then offer it again. Sometimes several repeated offerings of the bath are better than only one offering left in the cage for a long time. In any case, let the bird take its own time at this—as it will anyway, of course, for you cannot take it (as you would a puppy) and just douse it in, with the appropriate impatient expletive!

You do not need to purchase a special bird bathing receptacle, for any roughish—that is, not highly glazed —china or pottery or earthenware dishes, that are flat and shallow, make good bird baths. You will soon discover that when a bird becomes accustomed to one sort of bathing dish, it will refuse to bathe in another one of different shape. Do not give the bird cold water to bathe in, under the mistaken idea that harsh ice-cold water bathing will render the bird hardy. Birds maintain a very high body temperature (see page 86), hence the water should be warm, feel warm to the hand, that is; water that feels only slightly warm to the hand will feel decidedly cool to the bird. Warm the water for the bird bath even in hot weather. Never allow the bird to bathe in a cool room, or in a room that is the least bit drafty. When a bird's feathers are wet it is extremely sensitive to cold and drafts. During the bird's molting period it should not be allowed to bathe more than twice each week; and if it is being fed on color food (see page 41), then one bath a week is all it should have. In general, a female bird should not be allowed to bathe from the time of the hatching of the eggs until the young are four or five days old.

If your bird persistently refuses to bathe, and if the sight of the bath seems to frighten him, or causes him to retreat to a far corner of the cage, or make other suspicious motions, then put into the bottom of the bath some moist grit, but no water, and leave him alone for a while to investigate this mystery. Sooner or later he will hop into the moist grit and look about. After he seems convinced that this new piece of apparatus is harmless, then cover the grit only slightly with water, and leave him alone as before. Repeat this, adding a little more water each time, and soon he will be enjoying his bath in a natural way. Thereafter you will have no more trouble. You can then dispense with the grit entirely. But remember always not to coax your bird or hover over him, or fuss over him. Least done, soonest accomplished, is a modification of the old maxim, which holds true for birds as well as for humans. Be patient and leisurely with your little pet; leave him to himself in peace and quiet often; nervous, jerky, fussy people seldom make good bird fanciers. A comforting corollary to this statement is that caring for a pet bird often helps nervous jittery people to acquire a more placid habit of action.

Ten Rules for Maintaining Your Bird In Good Health

1. Keep your bird in a well ventilated room, where the air is clean and clear. Birds usually fall sick in a hot, vitiated, stuffy atmosphere; especially in an atmosphere of tobacco smoke, heavy frying odors, dust, or the fumes from gas stoves or portable oil heaters.
2. Do not hang the cage near bright lights, nor high up in a room where hot air accumulates.
3. Do not hang the cage in a draft, or in a cool portion of a room, or in a portion of the room where temperature changes are likely to take place rapidly.
4. Keep the cage in as quiet a place as possible; not in the midst of rollicking children or frisking dogs, or near to large rapidly moving or noisy objects, such as electric fans and blaring radios. Save your bird's delicate little ears from being assailed by loud, sudden, strident sounds.
5. Keep the cage out of direct sunlight, except for short periods of time, and even then provide a place for quick retreat into the shade.
6. Keep the cage scrupulously clean (see page 14).
7. See that the bird has bathing facilities offered it at least three times a week, or oftener if you prefer; except during the molting season, or when color food is being fed. (See page 41).
8. Don't overfeed your bird! This is very important indeed. Give it only the bird seed, and other suitable foods. Give these only in the minimum quantities.

And please don't try to tempt your bird's appetite with so-called dainties, such as candy, cakes, cookies and similar morsels. If you must indulge in these things, at least protect the digestive system of your helpless little feathery friend!

9. Don't worry your bird with too much fussy attention; let him have long periods each day of peace and quiet.

10. Don't dose your bird with this or that if you think he isn't acting quite like himself. Wait and see. All creatures even when in perfect health have their ups and downs, their periods of exuberance and their periods of relaxation. But if your bird really falls ill, and if the simple home remedies suggested in this chapter fail of their expected effect, then consult a veterinarian without delay.

Common Cage Bird Ailments and Their Treatments

The following catalogue of common ailments of small cage birds includes only those most frequently encountered, those whose symptoms are pronounced, easily recognized, and characteristic; and whose treatments are simple and usually easy to administer by the intelligent layman.

If your bird is suffering from any ailment whose symptoms are not understood, and which do not respond readily to the remedies suggested here, then you should consult a competent veterinarian without delay.

Bird lovers must guard against falling into the reprehensible practice of continually dosing their little charges with all sorts of recommended nostrums, under the impression that their birds are ill because their actions are not wholly understandable. One must keep in mind that bird physiology is in some respects quite different from human physiology, even though the fundamentals of digestion, assimilation, circulation, oxidation, egestion, excretion, respiration, tissue-formation, and the like, are essentially alike. Just to give some examples of this: the normal human body-temperature is about 98.6 degrees Fahrenheit; whereas the normal body temperature of a small songbird lies somewhere in the neighborhood of 106 to 112 degrees! Again, birds possess no diaphragm, no bladder, almost no salivary glands, almost no sense of either smell or taste; their lungs are far smaller than ours in proportion to their bodies; they possess large air sacs in the coelom, connected with the meagre lungs; their heartbeats and respiratory movements are far more rapid than ours.

Few persons, except trained veterinarians experienced in the intricacies of physiology and bird pathology, are able to diagnose correctly, or to treat understandingly, many of the problematical diseases of birds. Hence it is well to repeat: do not try to treat a sick bird beyond the mere attentions such as first aid to home birds implies. Try a few simple, harmless remedies; if these do not produce the desired results, go no farther. Usually it is better to rely on the wisdom and experience of a veterinarian at the outset. However, here are some suggestions, before we list specifically various bird maladies and their customary treatments.

General Procedures in the Care of Sick Birds

If one suspects that a bird is ailing, one should at once try to discover the cause of the ailment, and remove it, rather than promptly begin to administer medication. When a bird is becoming ill, regardless of the cause, it sits quietly on its perch crouched down, perhaps, and with its feathers all ruffled up looks like a puffy little ball. The lower it sits, the puffier its feathers appear, the more nearly closed are its eyes, the sicker it is. One can usually tell from the progress of these symptoms how ill the bird feels. In all this matter of diagnosing bird disease, one is forced to rely on appearance and analogy, for the birds have no speech with which to help us in our diagnosis.

One of the first procedures with an ailing bird is to remove it to a quiet, dimly lighted place, and give it a little extra warmth; sometimes, even in summer, a little extra warmth is necessary. Feed it upon a

CAGE BIRD AILMENTS AND TREATMENTS 21

bland soft diet, and allow it to nurse its woes alone for a time, watching it carefully in the meantime. During this observation period, a mild aperient may be given, for example Syrup of Buckthorn, five drops in a tablespoonful of water, or any other very gentle laxative. Give this even if there seems to be some looseness of bowels. Or put three drops of Syrup of Rhubarb in a tablespoonful of water, with three drops of honey. Put this into its drinking cup, and leave it there from three hours to a half a day. Watch the bird's actions when at rest; note its breathing, whether forced, labored, wheezy, light and spasmodic, etc. Examine the droppings to see if they are hard, scant or stringy, or unusually loose and watery. Notice whether there are discharges from the eyes, nostrils, or beak, or whether there is any trace of blood from these parts or from the vent. Does the bird cough or sneeze, or click its bill frequently, or droop its wings? All these are signs of ailments which will presently be discussed in some detail.

Often a sick bird will respond to a simple change of food, or to a lighter diet, or to a quieter situation, or to a little more warmth, or to a long period of repose induced by covering its cage with a light cloth. Some such simple measures as these will often be quite enough to restore a mildly ill bird to health; sometimes quiet and a little extra warmth will do it.

In feeding a sick bird, be unusually careful that the food is fresh and pure; discard any seeds or substance that may be in the least stale, rancid or musty. Be sure that the water in the drinking cup is fresh; change it frequently, washing the drinking cup each time. Use distilled water in the drinking cup with the medicine. If you cannot get distilled water, then use only water which has been filtered, then boiled for fifteen minutes, then allowed to cool.

If green food, such as water cress, for example, is

used, it should be carefully picked over and all discolored leaves discarded. The plant should then be washed thoroughly, and thoroughly dried, either by shaking and then hanging up for a few minutes, or by pressing between absorbent sheets of paper towels or paper napkins. Some persons prefer old clean linen. If fruits are used, or such vegetables as carrots, take only those parts which are firm and fresh, and, as with the green foods, never offer them to the bird without first being dried. That is, never feed a cage bird fresh foods that are wet and dripping.

If it becomes advisable to administer medicines to an ailing bird, these are best given in drinking water, or in many cases sprinkled on soft food, such as a bit of bread moistened with milk. A veterinarian probably will prefer to give liquids in the beak by means of a medicine dropper, but this is an awkward procedure for a novice to undertake. However, if you know how to hold a bird while giving it medicine direct by mouth, then use a hollow quill to which a small rubber bulb has been attached. Or if you insist on using a glass medicine dropper, see that the tip of the dropper is melted perfectly smooth in a bunsen flame; otherwise it will scratch or even lacerate the very soft membranes of the bird's mouth. Administering medicines in the beak with a dropper usually results in the bird being subjected to a good deal of nervous excitement during the struggling process, an excitement which can do the bird no good in its ailing condition. It is far better, I think, to let the bird administer its own medicine in the drinking water, even if this method is not quite as accurate in its dosage.

I. Digestive System Ailments

Troubles in the digestive systems of cage birds arise in most cases through a lack of care of the food

CAGE BIRD AILMENTS AND TREATMENTS 23

and the drinking water. Their chief causes are: dirty drinking cups, foul drinking water, soured food substances, inferior seed supply, or lack of some of the essential foods, such as fresh seeds, fresh green food, fruits, carrots and other vegetables. One of the most fruitful causes of upsets is the feeding to the birds of strange and unnatural foods, such as cakes, cookies, candies, and so-called "dainties" to which the birds are entirely unaccustomed.

The following are the commonest of the digestive system ailments, and their suggested treatments. If the birds do not respond readily, then consult a veterinarian at once. Since bird metabolism is rapid, the progress of an illness may be rapid also.

Diarrhea

Symptoms: Droppings very liquid, frequent, and ill smelling.

Treatment: Give a mild aperient, to remove any irritating matter from the digestive tract. With-hold green foods for a few days, and supply the bird with poppy (maw) seed and with crushed cuttlefish bone. This will usually correct the complaint, unless it be an obstinate one. If no improvement is manifest, give a piece of bread moistened with milk, over the surface of which has been dusted some bismuth (subnitrate). Into one ounce of water in the drinking cup put three or four drops of laudanum. If possible, put two drops of olive oil directly into the beak.

Dysentery

Symptoms: Bird very listless, refusing to take food but drinking a great deal of water, and giving indications from time to time of suffering griping pains. The droppings are thin, and mingled with much mucus and blood.

Treatment: Give the bird extra warmth, even if it be summer. Put him entirely on a diet of bread well softened with milk; add to the latter about five or six drops of pure paraffin oil, sprinkled with ordinary canary seed. If this does not effect a cure, give the bird from two to five drops of laudanum, preferably in the beak, every morning for three or four days. Add twelve drops of brandy to the water in the drinking cup each morning.

Constipation

Symptoms: The bird sits around in a listless way, refusing to take food. The evacuations are few and scant, and, in evacuating, the bird makes spasmodic jerky movements, showing obvious distress.

Treatment: In ordinary cases, and these may be frequent, it will probably be sufficient to administer about ten drops of glycerine in the drinking water for a day or two; at the same time give liberally of apple, lettuce, chickweed and similar green leafy foods. If no improvement is seen after two days, then add a pinch of Epsom salts to the drinking water. Do not give castor oil to cage birds.

Indigestion

Symptoms: The bird sits on its perch with its head tucked away in its feathers; when roused for feeding, it pecks listlessly and fussily at the food, cracking the seeds and then rejecting both the husk and the kernel.

Treatment: Bread and milk, with 5 drops of liquid paraffin; also 6 drops syrup of rhubarb and sodium sulphate the size of a small pea in one ounce of drinking water. Administer all the above for 2 or 3 days.

Bound Gizzard or Impaction

Symptoms: Constipation, with a swollen and hard lumpy feel below the breastbone of the bird.

Treatment: Reduce the food supply, and give bread softened with milk and sprinkled with poppy seeds. Give plenty of lettuce, water-cress, pears, grapes, oranges. Put from one to six drops (according to the size of the bird) of olive oil in the beak each day for three or four days. Into the drinking cup put a solution consisting of one ounce of water in which has been dissolved a crystal of sulphate of soda about the size of a small pea. Continue this treatment until it can be seen that the bird is feeling like its old self, and until the bowel movements are normal.

II. Respiratory Ailments

The common ailments of the respiratory system are colds, huskiness of voice, catarrh, asthma and pneumonia. These are induced by allowing the bird to be subjected for long periods of time to cool or cold drafts of air, or by keeping the bird in a place where sudden temperature changes are likely to occur. In the incipient stages of these ailments the bird sits very much crouched down on its perch, all fluffed up into a little ball of feathers, and at intervals shivers, coughs or sneezes. This is followed by the breath coming rapidly and spasmodically, often accompanied with wheezing or squeaking, and labored effort.

Common Colds

Symptoms: Feathers fluffed out into a ball; bird coughs or sneezes, and there is a slight discharge at the nostrils. The droppings are usually whitish and watery.

Treatment: Dissolve one teaspoonful of Epsom salts in a pint of well boiled water, or distilled water. Put this in the drinking cup for two or three days. Or this may be varied by adding to the water in the drinking cup fifteen drops of a solution composed of equal parts of glycerine, honey and lemon juice. Give bread softened with milk onto which has been dropped two drops of cod-liver oil, the whole sprinkled over with powdered or confectioner's sugar. If the bird refuses this, sprinkle it liberally with poppy seed. Place a piece of soft red pepper in the cage near the drinking cup. Give plenty of green foods and keep the bird warm and quiet. Some bird fanciers recommend a teaspoonful of whiskey in the water of the drinking cup as a temporary and immediate relief measure, if the bird seems to be unusually miserable.

Huskiness, Wheeziness, or Loss of Voice

This is apt to develop into a serious complaint unless dealt with at once. It is often neglected, especially as the condition makes its appearance in a rather simple huskiness in the voice, at first scarcely perceptible. It is brought on by the bird being left in a cool draft, or by being suddenly transferred from a warm place to a cool one. It attacks the most vigorous singing types of birds, especially the Roller Canaries.

Treatment: Begin by putting from three to five drops of glycerine in the water of the drinking cup, and covering the cage with a cloth to prevent the bird using its voice. In the meantime give only plain bird seed mixture and a piece of bread, moistened with milk, onto which has been dropped two or three drops of emulsion of cod-liver oil and two drops of olive oil. Sprinkle the whole lightly with confectioner's

CAGE BIRD AILMENTS AND TREATMENTS

sugar. Give the bird a little extra warmth for two or three days. If the attack is a light one the bird should be all right in about three days' time; if it is not, then take it to a veterinarian without delay, for if this condition is neglected it may result in the serious impairment, or even total loss, of the bird's voice.

Catarrh

Symptoms: The bird is more or less fluffed up, according to the severity of the attack, shows a thin watery discharge from the nostrils, and sometimes moves the head from side to side in obvious irritation.

Treatment: For this trouble, equal parts of laudanum and glycerine are often indicated; but it is recommended that this be administered in the beak by a veterinarian. Keep the bird slightly warmer than usual and give plenty of green foods: lettuce, watercress, Swiss chard, etc.

Asthma

Symptoms: The bird sits all fluffed up on its perch, its head sometimes depressed, sometimes elevated, its beak slightly open, its breathing difficult, often wheezy or squeaky.

Treatment: Put daily into the drinking cup a solution of two drops of iodine in two ounces of distilled or well boiled water. Give a mild aperient every second day for a week or ten days. Give also bread, well softened with milk, onto which has been dropped two drops of a mixture consisting of equal parts of cod-liver oil emulsion and syrup of iodide of iron. A little honey may be applied with a soft feather to the inside of the throat, and a little Mentholatum in each nostril. After a time place in the drinking cup a liquid made by steeping in a cupful of water a teaspoonful of flaxseed. Bring the water to a boil, pour in the seed, and let the infusion stand and draw until cool. Put in the cage, on the wires, a piece of raw salt pork in a place where the bird can get at it easily.

This ailment is often chronic, and is seldom wholly curable, though much can be done for the relief and comfort of the fluffy little sufferer. Sometimes overfeeding causes a bird to exhibit symptoms similar to those of asthma. Try restricting the diet of your bird for a few days, and the symptoms may abate. In true asthma give a plain, easily assimilated diet. Some kinds of foods aggravate an asthmatic condition; try and discover what foods do this in the case of your particular bird, and eliminate them from its diet.

Pneumonia

Symptoms: These usually appear very suddenly. They are, a rapid and difficult respiration, effected with the beak partly open; the feathers much fluffed out; the wings often drooping and tremulous. Often the beak is gritted or clicked as the bird labors in breathing; there may be some slight catarrhal discharge as well. Weakness quickly ensues, and the bird falls from its perch and dies in the course of a few hours or a couple of days at the most. Recovery, however, sometimes takes place.

Treatment: Take the bird to the veterinarian at once, if the symptoms are those of undoubted pneumonia, for this is a very serious condition indeed. But first the bird should be quickly put in a quiet, warm, even hot situation, in order that it may become thoroughly warmed through. This will often temporarily relieve and revive the bird. A druggist will make up for you the following formula, which may be administered in water if the bird lives and revives enough to drink: Liquor ammonia acetate, 3 parts; tincture

CAGE BIRD AILMENTS AND TREATMENTS 29

squills, 3 parts; sweet spirits nitre, 2 parts; simple syrup, 5 parts. Place five drops of this in the drinking water twice daily, fresh water and a new dosage being used each time. This, however, may be administered in the beak, undiluted, two or three drops twice daily, but it is better to refrain from handling or alarming a bird afflicted with pneumonia. Once pneumonia has been established, take the bird promptly to a veterinarian; exercise especial care not to subject it to a chill.

III. MISCELLANEOUS AILMENTS

Septic Fever, Bird Fever, Bird Plague

Symptoms: Bird thin and emaciated, even though it may be feeding normally, or even show an unusual appetite; sitting a great deal of the time all huddled up on its perch with its feathers much fluffed out, not hitching about, but motionless, as though avoiding all unnecessary exercise. (For Parrot Fever, or Psittacosis, see page 73).

Treatment: The first thing to do, if you have other birds, is to isolate a fever-sick bird at once, for septic fever is highly contagious. If the attack is a severe one, there is usually little that can be done, as the bird will quickly die. A veterinarian should be consulted at once; in the meantime, dissolve a piece of copper sulphate about the size of half a pea in a pint of distilled water, or well boiled water, and put this into the drinking cup.

If cages and water supply are perfectly clean and sanitary, and if clean, uncontaminated, unspoiled foods are used, septic fever will very rarely make its appearance.

Sweating, or Nervousness

Symptoms: This condition often occurs in hens that are raising a nestful of young, and is characterized by dullness or listlessness on the part of the bird. The breast feathers are sodden and matted, and since this looks like sweating, it is called so. This condition, however, is brought about by the watery diarrhoeic evacuations of the young birds, soaking the hen's feathers as she sits.

Treatment: This is for the young birds. Empty and clean the drinking and food cups, and thoroughly clean the cage. Reduce the amount of bread or cracker crumbs in the egg food you have been feeding the young, and into the egg food put one teaspoonful of arrowroot powder to a teaspoonful of the egg food. Sprinkle the whole with poppy seed before offering it to the birds. Now make a solution of one teaspoonful of lime water in an ounce of distilled or well boiled water and put this in the drinking cup every day until the condition of the young birds' bowels is normal again, as will be indicated by the breast feathers of the hen returning to their normal condition.

Fits, or Epilepsy

If one is so unfortunate as to possess a bird which is subject to fits, it is advisable to chloroform the poor little sufferer at once. If kept alive, not only is its existence one of misery to the bird, but its owner is repeatedly subjected to the sorrow of seeing his little pet periodically forced to undergo this torture; with no hope of permanent recovery.

The very best way to put a bird peacefully to sleep in one's home, where chloroform or ether are not readily available, is to take a small cardboard box, punch a dozen or so large holes in the cover, with a

CAGE BIRD AILMENTS AND TREATMENTS

large pencil, and about two dozen in the bottom of the box. Place the bird in the box, secure the cover tightly—perhaps with Scotch tape—and put it over a large gas burner. Turn on the gas (of course without lighting it!), and in less than a minute the bird will fall peacefully asleep. If you have chloroform or ether at hand, place the bird in a tight small box, and then through a small hole in the cover introduce a few squirts of the ether or chloroform with a medicine dropper. Again, in less than a minute, peaceful sleep will supervene. Do not place cotton in the box, as this prevents the rapid volatilization of the chloroform; the more rapid is the volatilization, the quicker is the terminal sleep.

In somniferating a pet bird (to use a friend's euphemism), be assured that almost at once the bird is stupified, and feels no pain, or hardly any discomfort, before its transition into the bird Valhalla.

Apoplexy, Stroke, Shock

Apoplexy causes death in a surprising number of cage birds. There are no premonitory symptoms, and usually there is nothing you can do. A bird may be sitting on its perch quietly, or singing, or preening its feathers, apparently in the best state of health and vigor, when it suddenly falls to the floor of the cage, makes a few spasmodic motions, and expires.

Apoplexy in birds, as shock in humans, frequently occurs after too prolonged and too heavy feeding; a bird that is stuffed with food, and overweight, is very apt to die at an early age from this malady. Or even if the bird survives, too heavy overeating develops masses of fatty tissue among the visceral organs, so that not only is their normal function impeded, but the blood stream is interfered with in its capillaries.

To keep apoplexy at bay, see that your bird has a

light but adequate diet, with plenty of fresh green foods, and that its bowels are in good condition at all times. Strictly avoid overfeeding. Keep the bird's bowels open; if any tendency to constipation shows itself, give a mild aperient in the drinking water, especially during the warm months of the year.

Cataract

Symptoms: The bird seems unable to guide its motions accurately, and gives evidence of poor sight. The pupils of the eyes, instead of being dark, look like little milky spots in the center of the diaphragm.

Treatment: A veterinarian should be consulted at once. There is no home treatment.

Sore or Inflamed Eyes

Symptoms: Inflamed reddish lids and eyes; the bird rubbing the sides of its head against its perch, or the wires of the cage, etc.

Treatment: Wash the eyes with warm boracic acid water, the same kind which the druggist puts up for human use. They may then be anointed with a mixture consisting of two drops of castor oil and one drop of Adrenalin Ointment No. 1 (obtainable at most large drug stores). Mix this thoroughly; it may be diluted with a drop or two of thin paraffin oil. Warm it before application. Or, if this cannot be readily had, use a 10 per cent solution of argyrol. Some recommend merely pure castor oil. Use these ointments or oils only if the boracic acid wash fails to be effective. Often the acid wash is all that is needed.

Sore Feet

Birds often suffer from sore feet, usually brought about by unclean or rough perches, or by bad conditions on the floor of the cage. The symptoms are easily recognizable.

Treatment: Wash the feet daily with a very warm solution of one teaspoonful of boracic acid powder dissolved in half a cupful of water, and then anoint them with zinc oxide ointment (obtainable in a tube at any drugstore). If the ointment as it comes from the tube is thick and stiff, dilute it with paraffin oil, or olive oil. Unless there is an infective condition, the trouble should disappear in a few days. If it does not, examine the condition of your perches before any further medication is given. This should be done at the outset, as perhaps rough perches, etc., are causing the complaint, or perhaps a dirty cage bottom. Therefore, while pursuing the treatment with the boracic acid, examine these parts of the cage carefully. Remove the tray at the bottom of the cage, wash and disinfect it thoroughly, then put in fresh, dry, soft pine sawdust for a time (with no grit). Change the perches; put in perches made of soft wood; white pine is best. See that the perches are fastened so that they do not turn or wobble as the bird shifts its position. The perches should not be shiny smooth, but feel softly rough, so that the birds do not have to grip them by main strength to prevent their toes slipping around. If your bird is in the habit of whittling its perches, then renew these as often as necessary. Do not anoint the perches themselves with any curative ointment, as this may cause them to become too slippery for the bird's comfort.

If the bird's feet continue to remain sore, bathe them with a warm seventy per cent solution of alcohol, and anoint them with the zinc oxide ointment. Sometimes this condition requires a week or so to clear up completely.

Egg Binding

This is a fairly common complaint among hens that have not had sufficient exercise (another reason for keeping a pet bird in a large cage); or that have had an insufficiently rounded diet. It should not make its appearance among carefully kept birds.

Symptoms: The bird sits disconsolately all huddled up on its perch, and makes frequent visits to the nest, without any egg appearing afterwards. After a time she may begin to show signs of distress and pain; weakness follows, and she may collapse, and be found in this condition either in the nest or on the floor of the cage. At the very outset of the distress the bird sits with her feet wider and wider apart; it seems as if she were trying to press her abdomen against the perch.

Treatment: Note this well: neither castor oil nor any laxative is to be administered. Put into the beak of your bird a few drops now and then of a mixture of equal parts of gin and water, and consult a veterinarian, unless you feel competent to deal with the situation yourself. In the latter case, apply the following treatment:

After having given a dose of the gin and water mixture, hold the bird for three or four minutes over a dish of hot water from which a gentle steam is arising —NOT however over a dish of actively boiling water. Then gently insert into the bird's vent the tip of a feather which has been dipped in warm olive oil, turning the feather round and round so as to lubricate thoroughly the mucous walls of the vent just inside the aperture. Then place the bird back in its cage, or directly on the nest, and the egg will usually be extruded within a few minutes' time.

Or you may wrap a damp, warm towel around the bird's body, and place it on a warm hot-water bottle.

CAGE BIRD AILMENTS AND TREATMENTS 35

The heat applied to the bird should be in excess of 100 degrees Fahrenheit, that is to say it should feel very warm to the hand, for the bird's normal temperature, remember, is somewhere in the range of 108 degrees or so. After this treatment, use the oily feather as before, and the bird will usually lay her egg. Some bird fanciers recommend using a glass medicine dropper for the insertion of the oil; this is satisfactory if one sees to it that no air bubble is introduced into the vent.

IV. BIRD ACCIDENTS

Dislocations

Dislocation of toe joints, or others, are at once apparent, and usually caused by birds dashing about the cage and catching their feet in some crevice or other. Such dislocations should be treated by a veterinarian, who is skilled in making anatomical readjustments of this kind.

Fracture of the Leg (Broken Leg)

In the case of a fracture of the leg, a small wooden splint, wound with cotton, may be applied, and held in place with small strips of surgeon's plaster. Leave the splint on for about sixteen days, or three weeks if possible, and then remove entirely. In the case of a fracture of the lower leg, or tarsus, take a quill from a chicken wing-feather, or pigeon's feather; split it, and then clasp it over the leg of the bird. The tarsus should first be lightly and thinly wound with a soft cotton thread. The split-quill splint may be held together either with fine thread, or thin strips of surgeon's plaster. When removing surgeon's plaster, touch it with a drop of chloroform from a medicine dropper. This liquifies the adhesive material of the plaster, and makes its removal easy, without any pulling. Threads are easier to remove, but they hold less securely than the plaster.

Fracture of the Wing (Broken Wing)

Broken wings should be allowed to heal without any external appliances, unless placed there by a skilled veterinarian. Remove all high perches from the cage, and place food and water on its floor. Isolate the bird, and keep it warm, shaded and quiet, to reduce its motions to a minimum.

Wounds

The tyro should not attempt to treat a severely wounded bird; it should be taken to a veterinarian at once. A severely wounded bird's troubles are usually attended to by a Higher Power; but if the bird is only slightly cut or abraded, the injured part may be treated to stop the bleeding at once with a solution composed of tannin, one part; benzoic acid from the gum, one part; collodion, twenty parts. Have some of this made up by the druggist in case of an emergency. This is to be applied to the bleeding part with a soft camel's hair brush. Hold the bird firmly for a moment after applying the solution, until the sting passes away, which it will do in about seven or eight seconds. A second application may be used after a few seconds, without injury. In about a minute or so, apply a bit of zinc oxide ointment, which may be softened with a drop or so of olive oil if too thick and stiff—though this latter treatment is not essential. After bleeding has stopped, return the bird to its cage; cover the cage with a cloth, and put it in a warm quiet place.

CAGE BIRD AILMENTS AND TREATMENTS 37

Overgrown Claws

In their natural state, all birds, by their constant activities, wear down the tips of their claws as fast as they grow out from the base; but in captivity, the claws, since they miss most of this compensatory abrasion, grow apace, and soon get in the bird's way, and catch on the perches or wires as the bird hops about. This is not only a matter of great discomfort to the bird, but a danger as well, as a snagged claw may cause a dislocation or breakage of the slender leg. These extra long curved claws should be trimmed every few months, or as often as is deemed necessary for the comfort of the bird. This trimming may be done with a pair of fine sharp scissors; great care being exercised to cut the claw far enough ahead of its principal blood-vessel to prevent bleeding. Should bleeding occur, touch the end of the bleeding claw with the collodion solution mentioned in the foregoing paragraph. About one third of an overgrown claw may be safely cut away without severing a blood vessel; in most cases nearly half of the claw may be cut.

Overgrown Bill

The horny jaws of a bird are covered with a tough, horn-like growth or envelope known as the bill, or rhamphotheca. This often becomes overgrown, thick, or distorted through lack of the proper amount of abrasion to keep it worn down. If such is the case, the horny bill may be trimmed with a very sharp small knife, much as one would trim thick fingernails. This is much better than to try to use a fine file, as the rasping process is very disagreeable to birds.

Feather Loss and Baldness

If a bird's plumage begins to come out, without any indication that the bird is infested with mites or lice, or that it is plucking out its own feathers, or that it is being plucked out by another bird, then a veterinarian should be consulted, for loss of feathers may be due to one or more obscure causes.

Birds which are in feeble health often develop scanty head feathers, and may become quite bald. This may be remedied, and in many cases cured entirely, by supplying extra warmth during the period of the natural molt, and by giving the bird plenty of green leafy food such as lettuce, water-cress, and the like, and apples. Also, every three days, give the bird a piece of bread, softened with milk, over which has been lightly sprinkled a mixture of one part of potassium chlorate and two parts of powdered sulphur. Get a tube of carbolized vaseline at the druggist's, and rub a little on the bare spots. With this may be mixed a little boracic acid ointment, and olive oil, to make a very soft mixture. Use sparingly.

Some cases of baldness occur through the habit of a companion bird in the same cage picking the feathers. In such a case the remedy is obvious. Separate the birds.

Occasionally loss of feathers is due to the presence of ectoparasites.

Parasites

Birds in a cage are frequently parasitized by ectoparasites, that is, parasites living on the outside of the skin. Two sorts of these, lice and mites, cause a great deal of trouble, but are easily eradicated.

The mites are extremely small, almost microscopic creatures belonging to the order *Arachnida* (spiders, scorpions, mites, king-crabs, etc.). They are white or grayish little specks with eight short legs. When a mite sucks up the blood of a bird, its body swells and becomes bright red. Hence these parasites are usually known as red mites. They are not normally red; only so after they have engorged a full meal. Mites feed only during the night, except in cases of very severe infestation. During the day they conceal themselves in crevices, such as the slits at the end of the wooden perches, cracks or nail holes in any wooden portions of the cage, under objects, especially under the metal cap at the top of a hanging cage, and in other hiding places. Sometimes they may be seen by the aid of a reading glass, or hand lens. To kill them, apply kerosene oil to all these places in which they are lurking, using a camel's hair brush for the purpose. The best method of extermination, however, is to immerse the entire cage for five minutes in actively boiling water. Many pet and bird stores carry mite and louse powders which are also satisfactory.

One can best remedy the mite problem on the body of the bird itself by furnishing the bird with Quassia water instead of ordinary water in its bath. Quassia water is made by putting two tablespoonfuls of Quassia, or Bitterwood chips, into a quart of actively boiling water. After the chips have been thoroughly stirred up in the boiling water, take the decoction from the fire and allow it to cool to room temperature. Then pour off the clear liquid from the top and add four tablespoonfuls of the decoction to a quart of water, for the bath.

The louse which usually parasitizes cage birds is the Gray Bird Louse, an insect, not a spider-relative like the mites. It does not feed on the blood or any other living tissue of the bird, but on its feathers. As it feeds, and moves about on the body of the bird, its sharp claws irritate the bird's skin, and cause great discomfort and itching. The eggs of this louse are firmly attached to the feathers, and their removal is difficult. However, the pest can be successfully combatted by blowing insect powder (usually pyrethrum) into the plumage of the bird with a small blower. Pet stores deal in insect powders which are sold with directions for their use. Insect powders are usually blown into the feathers every four or five days or so, for several weeks, to insure the killing of the young as they emerge from the eggs at intervals. After a short period of this regularly spaced treatment the lice will usually all have been destroyed.

Sometimes, in cleaning the floor of the cage, one notices fragments of soft worms in the droppings of the birds. When these are detected remedial measures should be started promptly. Stir eight or ten drops of tincture of gentian in an ounce of distilled or freshly boiled water, and place this in the drinking cup for two or three days; in the meantime give two drops of olive oil daily. This may be administered in the bill with a medicine dropper, or placed on a small bit of bread moistened with milk. If the bird refuses this, sprinkle a few fine seeds over it. In giving medicine on bread, it is often well to increase the dosage very slightly, as sometimes the bread is not all eaten, some of it being scattered over the bottom of the cage. Another treatment for worms is to keep the bird on a fast for about three hours, and then feed it a piece of bread, well moistened with milk, and dusted over with freshly ground areca (betel) nut. After this has been eaten, in about half an hour offer its customary food and fill the drinking cup with the gentian solution. Repeat this treatment three or four times. This should rid the bird of these distressing endoparasites. If it does not, with-hold the treatment for a day or so, and then repeat it.

Treatment of Birds During the Molting Period

During the natural time of your bird's molt, give it a little extra warmth, and a full, well-balanced diet. Besides the usual food, supply the bird from time to time, or perhaps every third day, with a piece of bread, well moistened with milk, and over it sprinkle a mixture consisting of potassium chlorate, one part, and powdered sulphur, two parts. If the bird refuses this, sprinkle it well with poppy seeds, or the seeds of the Common Plantain, or Rattails, or White Man's Foot (*Plantago major*). Also give in the food, every day, plenty of apple, lettuce, water-cress, or any of the usual green leafy foods that you have been using. If your bird does not take green leafy food readily at this time, try him with some of the soft green leaves of cabbage. Most birds will take this when they are finicky about other green foods. Or you may vary the leafy diet with leaves of Swiss chard, or mustard leaves, or beet greens, or radish tops. Always bear in mind that these green leafy foods must be thoroughly washed, and thoroughly dried before being offered to the bird.

If baldness sets in at this time—as it sometimes does—be especially careful of infections of any kind in the food, for the bird is probably not in its pink of condition and is likely to pick up disease easily. To be sure that no infections lurk in the leafy foods, they might be washed in boiled water in which has been dissolved a little potassium chlorate. Dissolve a few crystals of this substance in the water until it becomes a very faint yellowish color, like extremely weak tea. Dry very thoroughly before feeding. If the bird seems unusually debilitated, feed it a piece of bread, moistened with milk, onto which have been dropped two drops of compound syrup of hypophosphites. Or one may administer a bit of bread moistened with milk as before, onto which have been dropped four drops of a mixture composed of syrup of iodide of iron and emulsion of cod-liver oil; equal parts. Keep the bird quiet, during the molting period.

If your bird's molt seems to be going forward normally, and no especial remedial measures seem called for, you might try feeding the bird with some of the foods especially recommended during the molt, other than those which form the full and well-balanced diet of the healthy bird. These are, to name the chief ones: flaxseed, chopped sunflower seeds, poppy seeds, and the Broad-Leaved Plantain already mentioned. These should be put into the cage on their long spikes, just as you gather them in the field; the birds like to tweak them off themselves.

The wild seeds should be thoroughly ripe and dry on their spikes. After you have gathered them, hang them up for a few days in a warm dry place and allow them to ripen and dry out.

If something seems to be going very much amiss in your bird's molting, and the feathers have stopped their shedding, and the bird acts uneasy and uncomfortable, then the bird has become, as the phrase has it, "stuck in the molt," and remedial measures will have to be taken. The best single remedy for the condition of stuck-in-the-molt, and one which will often all alone reestablish the molting mechanism is to support the cage over a large dish of actively steaming, *but not actively boiling* water, covering the cage and the whole steaming apparatus with

TREATMENT OF BIRDS DURING MOLTING PERIOD 43

a large bath towel or thick fabric of some sort. Let the bird stay in this warm moist atmosphere for eight to ten minutes, peeking in once in a while to see how he is faring. Then gradually—not quickly—remove the towel, and allow the cage and bird to come back to room temperature slowly. Keep the cage in a very warm room while all this is going on, and be careful afterwards to prevent any sudden change in temperature, or any drafts of cool air. Birds are especially sensitive to drafts during their molting period.

When the molt is over your bird should gradually resume its old energetic and sprightly ways, and begin to sing again with its accustomed vigor. If it does not, then recourse might be had to some of the simple tonics we have mentioned, but stop all medicinal adjuncts just as soon as you can. It is very easy at this time to fall into the habit of becoming a "doser." Don't use any medicines unless you clearly see that they are needed. Warmth and quiet are the two best medicines for birds at all times. Always try these first!

How to Tell the Sex and Age of Cage Birds

If you wish to purchase a male canary, or other small singing cage bird, go to a reputable dealer, who will usually show you the leg-band on the bird, telling its sex, and will also give you a statement that the bird is the sex you desire. It is difficult to determine the sex of a bird from the anatomy alone. The conclusive evidence for the sex of a bird is found in the external form, or morphology, of the vent. In the male, the cloacal aperture, as the vent is called, is carried on the apex of a low elevation, or rounded bulge, which is directed slightly backwards. This elevation is not very pronounced except during the mating season, when, in some birds, it swells out into quite a pronounced papilla. The cloacal aperture of the female, on the other hand, is carried on a low swollen area, which is almost on a level with the rest of the skin of the vent region.

The actions of the two birds are often quite accurately diagnostic; the cock will act "cocky," quick in its motions, energetic, alert, hopping about with a bouncing resilience of limb, as if he were mounted on springs, aggressive, even bullying in its demeanor, saucy. The hen, on the other hand, will be quieter in her actions, more sedate, just serenely hopping about, chirping now and then, perhaps.

The songs of the two sexes will also help in the identification of sex; the male, of course, being the

HOW TO TELL SEX AND AGE OF CAGE BIRDS

chief performer. This alone will often distinguish between them.

The mating actions, as everyone would recognize, marks the male and the female.

Small cage birds, like canaries and others, may be judged as to age fairly well by the condition of the legs and feet. In young birds the skin and scales covering the legs and feet are smooth, glossy and unwrinkled. The scales of the tarsus, and on the toes are regular, smooth, neither curled up nor scuffed, nor thickened at the edges. In old birds these structures we have mentioned are roughened, scuffed up, thickened, sometimes distorted, and look plainly old and worn. Again, the claws of young birds are long and finely pointed and delicate, whereas those of old birds are rough, thick and blunt, and may indeed be very blunt due to trimming. Close attention to these points will tell much as to the relative ages of birds. They will not, of course, indicate just how many years old the birds may be. Old birds will not act with the same sprightliness, alertness, activity and grace of younger birds. In the matter of exact age in years of a bird, you will have to trust your bird dealer.

Length of Life of Cage Birds

In a state of nature, and barring accidental deaths, our small native songbirds live from eight to twelve years on the average; but with cage birds this life span is quite apt to be longer, since the birds are under constant care, and their natural enemies have been removed. Dr. Alexander Wetmore (See Federal Government Bulletin referred to on page 114) says:

"Dr. C. W. Richmond, Associate Curator of Birds in the United States National Museum, relates that two birds (canaries) hatched in the same brood and kept entirely separated after they had left the nest, lived for eighteen years, and died within a few weeks of each other. Another case on record is of a canary known to have been at least thirty-four years old when it died, and it is believed that even this advanced age may have been exceeded. Usually, with the advance of the years, the birds molt irregularly, or lose a part of the feathers entirely. It is said that canaries which have not been paired live much longer than those which have been allowed to breed."

Birds which have been paired use up a good deal of their fund of life's energy in the production of sperms and eggs, and have further drains made upon their general systems. Many birds continue to lay eggs, if the eggs are removed from the nest, for a long time. The record for this seems to be a Flicker (Yellowhammer) which laid seventy-one eggs in seventy-three days;

a record which has been cited many times. It is not uncommon today to find especially developed domestic hens that will lay well over two hundred eggs in a single season.

The Mating and Breeding of Cage Birds

The mating and breeding of small home cage birds is a practice which would require, for adequate treatment, a whole book to itself. The beginner in this practice (or business, as it usually is with most persons who once make a start in it), should at the outset own two or three good comprehensive books on the subject. Suggestions for these books will be found in the Bibliography, beginning on page 111. Also the beginner should write to some of the periodicals on cage birds, whose special editors stand ready to help anyone engaging in the complicated business of bird breeding. Lists of these periodicals may be found on page 114 of this book.

While you are making up your mind as to the extent to which you wish to go in bird breeding, here are a few simple beginning suggestions.

When you have selected your pair of breeding birds, and have put them together, put the cage in a very quiet place, and watch the birds closely for a time. Should they seem more inclined to fight than to mate, transfer them to separate cages; put the cages close together, and leave them so for three or four days, or perhaps for a week. By this time the birds should have become accustomed to each other's company, at least. If, at the end of this time, the male seems to be eager to get through the bars of his cage, and into the cage of the female; and if the female, meantime, is beginning to flit her wings nervously now and then, or to flap them, and seems to be soliciting the attentions of

MATING AND BREEDING OF CAGE BIRDS

the bird in the other cage, then you may safely put the two birds together in one cage, when mating ought to ensue at once.

Breeding cages, well equipped with nest racks and all other necessities, can be had at any good bird store. All-metal cages are recommended, as these can be kept most sanitary, and are most easily disinfected and washed. Some fanciers do not put their birds into the breeding cages until they have been mated for several days. At the end of this time, the birds should begin to show some interest in making a nest, and now the nesting material should be provided. You will know when to provide this nesting material, for you will see the female bird flitting about carrying feathers in her bill, or a bit of any soft stuff she may have found; or you will see her poking here and there around the edge of the bottom of the cage as if looking for something that she had lost. This means that the urge for making a nest is beginning to make itself felt.

After a day or two, when she shows a serious intention of making a nest, give her a few bits of soft string, bits of cotton, slender soft blades of dried grass, a little dried moss, some few short horse hairs, dog hairs, goat hairs, etc. Do not give her great bunches of material at first. If the first rather meagre supply of nesting material is begun to be incorporated into a nest, then you might fasten against the side of the cage a small wire rack, containing larger quantities of the nesting materials. The nesting fibres should all be rather short. This is very important. Long horse hairs, or long pieces of string are dangerous, as they almost always, sooner or later, entangle the adults or the young.

Some people insist on building the nests for their cage birds themselves! This is not as foolish as it may seem, for frequently the birds just waste their time fussing around, carrying nesting stuff here and there, in the end making a very indifferent nest, or sometimes no nest at all. In fact, some females will refuse to build any nest, but will readily occupy a nest that has already been built for them.

Almost any good kind of a container or support may be put up for the birds to nest in, or on. Some use round, or half-round wire strainers. Others prefer an earthenware dish, and this is very good, as it can be easily cleaned. The rush or willow-woven nest pocket, sold by some dealers in bird supplies, may be good, but it makes an excellent place for the harborage of vermin, and is hard to clean. The nest box may be of wood, preferably a good hard wood. Hard wood is easy to keep clean. But whatever the nest box or support is, it should be fastened to the side of the cage about an inch or so above the perches, and about midway between them. Care must be exercised not to get the top of the nest box too near the top of the cage; leave plenty of room for going and coming. Likewise see to it that the nest is not too near the perches. If it is too near, the male bird is more likely to annoy the female during her times of quiet incubation. A little experimentation on the part of the birds' owner is always necessary here.

After the birds have been successful in their pairing the female will begin to lay eggs, the first one appearing usually in from ten to twenty-five days after the first fertilization. From three to six eggs will normally be laid.

If the hen shows distress during the egg-laying period, and seems to be unable to discharge an egg, she may be suffering from a common complaint known as egg-binding. Read the symptoms of this disorder, page 34.

As the eggs are laid, remove them with a teaspoon, and keep them in a dish of oatmeal, cornmeal or bran. When the female has completed her number, three

MATING AND BREEDING OF CAGE BIRDS 51

to six, replace them in the nest. The hen will then incubate them all at once; they will hatch almost at the same time. This will normally take about two weeks.

Some breeders strongly recommend the removal of the cock when the hen begins incubating the eggs. This surely should be done if it is apparent that he is annoying his mate. Some cocks are pestiferous, others are not; you will soon discover what kind of a mate you have provided for your bird, and can then act accordingly.

There is another reason for transferring the male to a separate cage at this time; for if he is left in the cage with an incubating female he gradually reduces his singing.

If your male bird does not annoy his mate, and you do not care especially whether he sings very much, then he should be left in the cage with her, for he will ordinarily assist her in the rearing of the family.

Watch the male bird as soon as the young begin to emerge from the egg, for at this time some birds develop the disagreeable habit of bullying the female and picking the feathers from the young birds. This habit may begin even before the first nestling has appeared, the male bird picking the feathers from his mate and adding them to the lining of the nest. Sometimes the female also develops this habit. To stop the procedure, furnish the cage plentifully with loose fluffy material, especially fluffy dried moss, soft cotton, etc., and be especially careful not to include pieces of string or horse hair, as the nestlings are apt to get such materials wound around their legs and necks.

The young will remain in the nest for some twenty-five days, more or less. After they have left it allow them to remain in the breeding cage and let the parent birds care for them until it is seen that the young are able to crack the tiny birdseeds themselves. Then remove them to a separate cage, and continue to feed the egg food to them (see page 54), gradually replacing it with the normal adult foods, seeds, green foods, etc., until the egg food has been entirely supplanted by the adult diet.

Since some birds, like canaries, may breed two or three times in a season, the hen may be ready for another brood when the young are finally taken away altogether, that is to say, in about twenty-five days or so. If the young of the first family are still unable to care for themselves, never mind. Give her some nesting material and let her begin a new nest if she wants to. If the male proves to be a normal father, he will assume the duties of bringing up the first batch of babies, while his mate prepares for the second batch.

The young birds should not be placed in a cage with older birds for some time. They must be very carefully watched during the first few days or weeks of their new independent life. If some of them do not seem able to feed satisfactorily for themselves, they should at once be put back into the cage with their parents. Some breeders put the young in a separate cage, close to the breeding cage, and allow the parent birds to feed the young through the wires. This is to be recommended only if the female develops the habit of picking out the feathers of the growing young, to supply nesting materials for relining the nest in preparation for the next brood.

Some Good Cage-Bird Foods

Reliable pet stores and bird stores carry full lines of foods recommended for cage birds. These can usually be relied upon. The following are some of the standard cage bird foods to be recommended.

INSECT FOOD, or MOCKINGBIRD FOOD. This is chiefly a mixture of dried ant eggs, dried insects, hemp meal, suet and miscellaneous dried, easily digestible vegetable substances. It is a very convenient, well-balanced, all-around food for the soft-billed birds, i.e., thrushes, troupials, nightingales, mockingbirds and the like. Birds of the finch family (*Fringillidae*), the so-called hard-billed birds, also take this food readily, as a useful adjunct to their usual seed diet.

BIRDSEED MIXTURE, GENERAL MIXTURE, or FINCH MIXTURE. Birdseed mixtures differ somewhat in their compositions, but in general the FINCH MIXTURE consists usually of red millet, one part; yellow millet, two or three parts; small yellow or white millet, three or four parts; and ordinary canary seed, two or three parts. This is the stock food for the hard-billed birds.

GREEN FOOD usually means any of the leafy foods useful for cage birds, such as water-cress, lettuce, Swiss chard, radish tops, spinach, cabbage, alfalfa, clover, curly dock, dandelions and the like. (See list of wild plants useful as bird foods, page 58.)

FRUITS. Any of the fresh fruits, such as apples, pears, oranges, and the like.

WILD PLANTS. See the list of wild plants useful as cage-bird foods, pages 58 to 60.

MILLET SPRAYS, or SPRAY MILLET. This is sold in the stores in the form of bouquets or sprays of the Indian Millet heads dried and tied into convenient little bunches, with the seeds in place. Birds like to pick the seeds off these sprays.

SEAWEEDS. Dried and finely ground kelp (a large marine alga known to botanists at Laminaria), also dried and ground Carrageen, or Irish Moss *(Chondrus crispus)*, the same plant which is so extensively used as human food. These dried seaweed granules are often blended with the egg food, or fed in other mixtures, and add very valuable elements such as iodine, and various minerals, to the bird's diet. Other marine algae (seaweeds) may also be used, such as dried sea-lettuce *(Ulva)*, the seaweed known as Laver; and I have been told that the very common rock-weeds, *Ascophyllum nodosum,* and *Fucus vesiculosus,* are also useful in the same way.

CHEESE. A plain simple whole milk cheese (but neither cream cheese, nor the fancy, highly flavored and spiced, packaged or canned or jarred or bottled cheeses) makes an excellent protein adjunct to the bird diet. Feed it as dry and crumbly as possible, neither in too hard nor too large lumps.

EGG FOOD. This is an old standard food, rich and fattening, but is not recommended for adult birds, unless they are on a special diet, as when in convalescence, or when being fed a color-food. It is chiefly a food for young birds, and used by many fanciers as the best all-around food for this purpose.

To prepare egg food, boil an egg hard, that is at least for twenty minutes, then mash the whole egg fine and smooth and add two rounded tablespoonfuls

SOME GOOD CAGE-BIRD FOODS

of thoroughly dried and finely crumbed whole-wheat bread. Crackers or toast may be used, also. Do not add milk or water to this mixture; it should be quite dry; mix it thoroughly with a fork and with the fingers. Some bird fanciers mingle a little commercial nestling food with the homemade egg food; this is recommended also.

CUTTLE BONE, or CUTTLEFISH BONE. This can be bought at any of the bird stores. It is the vestigial dorsal skeleton of the squid or cuttlefish, and is placed between the bars of the cage for the birds to pick at when they will. It is not just merely an abrasive for the birds' bills, as is sometimes said, but a valuable source of calcium carbonate in the birds' diet.

MEAL WORMS. These can be purchased in quantity from the pet stores and biological supply companies. They come packed in bran, which is their food supply as well. These meal worms are the larvae of the darkling beetle, *Tenebrio molitor.* They are very prolific, make an excellent and rich food adjunct and are especially relished by birds during their molting season.

COLOR FOOD. This is a preparation fed to birds to increase the brilliance of their plumage after a normal molt has taken place. The color food is begun to be fed just before they begin their molting and is continued through the molting period to its complete close, that is until the birds are again fully feathered. If one wishes to keep permanent the color thus produced, then one must give the color food to the bird regularly during every molting period; otherwise, if discontinued, the plumage will return to its normal duller color.

A simple color food for canaries is made by first preparing the egg food (as explained on page 54).

Then add to this (for each egg used) a half teaspoonful of good fresh, highly colored paprika and two or three drops of olive oil, or enough to form a good firm paste. Give a half teaspoonful of this paste every day until the feathers reach the desired color; then decrease the amount gradually until the end of the molt. If desired, the egg food and color food and olive mixture may also be mingled with any of the good commercial molting foods. While the color food is being fed to the birds, offer them also, mixed with the regular seed diet, about a fifth of the quantity, of flax seed. Keep the birds out of strong light, as this will fade the feather color.

GRIT. This is not a food, but is closely associated with the process of digestion. Hence listed here. Birds have no teeth, and the grinding action on the food in the gizzard is dependent largely on the grit present there. The grit supplied to birds should therefore be hard and fairly sharp. A good commercial grit usually contains such things as good quartz sand, shell, and also bone, sulphur, iron sulphate, a little salt, all ground to the proper size. Grit on the floor of the cage also helps to keep the birds' feet clean. It may be used clear, or mixed with a little pine sawdust, when used thus.

When birds have been imported from abroad, or have come from long distances, frequently the grit has been with-held and when birds first receive it after this privation, they often gorge themselves on it. Do not give your recently bought bird much grit at first. Use it sparingly, and watch your bird's feeding actions carefully for a few days.

Native Wild Plants as Sources of Cage-Bird Foods

It is not generally known that a very valuable source of food for cage birds is the large assemblage of native plants (or weeds and wild flowers) found so abundantly in our city parks, vacant lots, roadsides, fields and meadows. These yield both green leaf-foods, but also and perhaps more importantly, a copious seed supply.

There is no doubt that some birds are impaired in health and others even rendered sterile, or made the subjects of disfiguring maladies, largely through the use of improper foods. In speaking of the great value of wild plants as cage-bird foods, the famous English aviculturist, Richard Morse, writes:

"I do not of course suggest that the exact diet of a bird in the fields would be the best and most suitable for a bird in a cage . . . but there is every reason for believing that the addition of fresh vital foods, absolutely untampered with, to the usual diet of captive birds, is one of the safest and surest of all means for balancing a diet and keeping the birds in thoroughly sound and vigorous health."

A single example may be cited before we proceed to list the common wild plants, accessible to all, plants which yield valuable bird foods. All birds of the great finch family *(Fringillidae,* of which the canaries are the chief members among cage birds) relish inordinately the seeds of that most common of wild plants (weeds, to most people), the Broad-Leaved Plantain, or White Man's Foot *(Plantago major)*. This is the plant whose seed stalks the English very accurately call Rat-Tails. The writer has repeatedly seen our common wild Goldfinches in the field, sitting on these long spikes of seeds and weighing them down, while they strip off the seeds with great gusto.

Here then is a list of our very common wild plants, wild flowers they really are (though some call them weeds, a term somewhat disparaging in the popular view). These can be found abundantly in our fields, meadows, hillsides, along our roadways, lanes and paths; even in our own gardens and home grounds, and many of them are present in every city park and vacant lot. (If you wish to learn the names of these plants consult: Hausman, E. H., *Beginner's Guide to Wildflowers;* see page 113 of the Bibliography.)

One more word before we furnish the list of the plants; wild seeds are particularly relished by all cage birds during the molting season. Hence the seeds should be gathered and labelled, and some of them kept especially to be fed during molting. It will be discovered that some birds like one kind, and others another. The canaries are very fond of the Broad-Leaved Plantain, or White-Man's Foot mentioned before in connection with the wild Goldfinches; the Zebra Finches prefer the seeds of the Lady's Thumb *(Polygonum)* and of the Chickweeds *(Stellaria);* the Bullfinches prefer the larger seeds of the Docks.

Thirty Common Wild Plants Yielding Foods for Cage Birds

    1. Blackberry *(Rubus)*.
    2. Evening Lychnis, or White Campion *(Lychnis alba)*.
    3. Field Mustard, or Wild Mustard *(Brassica ar-*

NATIVE WILD PLANTS AS SOURCE OF FOOD

vensis). Also the White Mustard, Indian Mustard, and Black Mustard.
 4. Birdweed, or Common Chickweed *(Stellaria media).*
 5. Mouse-Ear Chickweed *(Cerastium vulgatum).* A very variable plant; as many as thirty or more distinct varieties have been described.
 6. Coltsfoot, or Coughwort *(Tussilago farfara).*
 7. Dandelion *(Taraxacum vulgare).*
 8. Curly Dock or Yellow Dock *(Rumex crispus).*
 9. Broad-Leaved Dock or Bitter Dock *(Rumex obtusifolius).*
 10. Meadow Grass *(Poa annua).*
 11. Rye Grass *(Lolium perenne).*
 12. Groundsel, or Grinsel *(Senecio vulgaris).*
 13. Mouse-Ear Hawk's Beard, or Mouse Bloodwort *(Hieracium pilosella).* Also other members of the genus *Hieracium,* such as the various hawkweeds and hawk's beards.
 14. Hawthorn *(Crataegus).* Birds greatly relish the large red fruits of the hawthorns. These hang on the trees for a long time, and may be gathered at all times. Even when dry and shrivelled they are very acceptable to the birds, for they dry rather than decay.
 15. Black Knapweed, or Star Thistle *(Centaurea nigra).*
 16. Scabious Knapweed *(Centaurea scabiosa).*
 17. Doorweed, or Prostrate Knotweed *(Polygonum aviculare).*
 18. Our Lady's Thumb or Heartweed *(Polygonum persicaria).*
 19. Meadowsweet, or Queen of the Meadow *(Spiraea latifolia).*
 20. Mountain Ash *(Pyrus aucuparia).* A tree, not a weed, and one used as an ornamental. The berries dry instead of decaying and may be used at any time.

21. Succory Dock, or Nipplewort *(Lapsana communis)*.

22. Broad-Leaved Plantain, or White Man's Foot *(Plantago major)*. One of the most useful and most copious of seed producers. Finches love the seeds still left on the spikes. They are especially valuable to birds during their molting periods.

23. Narrow-Leaved Plantain, or Ribwort *(Plantago lanceolata)*. Almost as useful as the Broad-Leaved Plantain.

24. Tansy, or Tansy Ragwort, or Stinking Willie *(Sebacio jacobaea)*. A very decorative plant, its bright yellow abundant flower-heads are very attractive in the fall garden.

25. Shepherd's Purse *(Capsella bursa-pastoris)*.

26. Sandwort, or Corn Spurry *(Spergula arvensis)*.

27. Common Teasel, or Gypsy Combs *(Dipsacus sylvestris)*. This is regarded as almost a medicine; its tonic effects are perceptible; must be fairly fresh (not over a few months old at most).

28. Yellow Rocket, or Winter Cress *(Barbarea vulgaris)*, and also the similar Scurvy Grass or Early Winter Cress *(Barbarea verna)*.

29. Common Sow Thistle *(Sonchus oleraceus)* and also the similar Field Sow Thistle *(Sonchus arvensis)*.

30. Water-cress *(Nasturtium officinale)*. Very valuable as a source of fresh green food.

When You Buy a Parrot

Parrots and their kin are in their best condition in warm weather, since they are tropical or semi-tropical birds. Always purchase a parrot in the warm months. There is then little danger of the bird being chilled during transportation. Carry the bird in a tight draft-proof box, preferably a thick-walled wooden one, without bars. When you arrive home, transfer the bird at once to its permanent cage, which should be, for parrots, preferably one with three wooden sides and a barred side. Cover this cage lightly with a cloth, and keep the bird warm and quiet for a few hours. Then remove the cloth gently—do not whisk it off suddenly—and let the bird accustom itself to its new surroundings. Do not crowd up close to the cage at first, or make rapid movements; and do not let several people press up close to the cage to examine the new pet. And keep quiet.

It is important to find out from the dealer, or from the former owner, what bird's diet was; keep it on the same diet for a few days, gradually changing over to the standard foods recommended for the species. If the bird seems to be in a rather run-down condition—that is, if it sits on its perch more or less fluffed up, or merely sits listlessly, and seems to lack alertness—then it should be fed for a few days on some soft and easily digested food, say boiled rice, or oats, or corn. At the same time a mild stimulant might be given for a day or two, about twelve or fifteen drops of brandy in the drinking water (a drinking cupful), or any mild tonic which is recommended. At such times, keep the bird carefully away from cool drafts, and at all times out of rooms filled with tobacco smoke, heavy frying odors, fumes from oil or gas stoves, and dust. Remove the bird from a room which you are dusting or sweeping. Also keep the bird away from very bright lights, hot stuffy places, or places where there is a good deal of noise and bustle.

Choosing a Parrot

Space will not permit here a detailed description of the various kinds of desirable parrots, but we will mention the kinds which for one reason or another, have proved the most popular with bird lovers. Some persons want a talking parrot, while others want only a bright colored and cozy little pet bird, and do not care whether it talks or not.

I. The Best Talkers

These are listed in the order of their ability and teachableness, but it must be remembered that opinions may differ slightly.

1. African Gray Parrot. Probably the best all-around parrot as far as vocal ability is concerned. It is conceded by nearly all to be the one which learns to sing and whistle best; though its talking abilities, while superb, are thought by others not to be of the very first quality.

2. Levaillant's Amazon Parrot.

3. Mexican Double Yellow-Head. This bird is said to possess a voice more nearly like the human voice —though this is a matter of opinion. However, the Yellow-Head is a superb talker, and by some is placed at the very head of the class. Another feature is that

WHEN YOU BUY A PARROT

it has a very gentle disposition; this cannot be said of all parrots.

4. Cuban Amazon Parrot.

5. Panama Parrot. These lovely green parrots are very teachable, and are valued by some more highly than any other parrot, for they combine extreme striking plumage with excellent talking ability. They are not quite such good singers and whistlers as the African Gray Parrot or the Mexican Double Yellow-Head.

6. Cuban Amazon, or Cuban Parrot. A strikingly colored bird; bright green with a red throat and white forehead. Only a second-rate talker, but a good whistler and singer and imitator of all kinds of sounds.

II. THE GENTLE AND QUIETER PARROTS

These make the best pets; they are affectionate and easily tameable.

1. Lovebirds. These are not the Shell Parakeets, or Budgerigars (though these birds are often called Lovebirds also), but are a sort of dwarf, chunky parrot; with large head and short tail. They look rather funny and top-heavy. These birds get along very amiably when there are several in a single cage, and are kept because they make such quiet domestic-acting little pets.

2. Shell Parakeets, or Budgerigars, or Budgies, sometimes also called Lovebirds, or merely Parakeets. There are some two hundred or more of these delicate graceful little parrot-like birds, with fat faces, short recurved bills and long slender tails; to say nothing of the delicate, striking colors. It would be useless to list more than a few of the more popular kinds here, for the choice is wide, and people's tastes in colors vary.

3. Blue Parakeets:

Cobalt Blue. Rather deep all-over color, with upper parts lighter.

Azure Blue. Upper parts whitish, under parts delicate pale blue.

4. Green Parakeets: The most popular of these is the Grass Green Parakeet, a lovely bright green bird, with its upper parts yellow.

5. Yellow Parakeets. The Canary Yellow Parakeet is by far the most popular member of the yellow group. The entire body of this bird is a bright canary yellow; but the tips of the wings are pure white; the tail is also white. There are green and red patches about the face.

6. White Parakeets. The White Shell Parakeet is the best of these. The entire body is white, with little bluish patches about the side of the head.

7. Mauve Parakeets. The Mauve Shell Parakeets are perhaps not as popular as the lighter, brighter colors; yet many people own them, to complete a color collection or for breeding. The upper parts are whitish, the lower parts mauve.

The above parakeets are the ones usually seen in dealers' establishments; but there are many others which one can buy, if one has the means to do so. The best way to determine what kinds of parakeets you wish to own is to consult a color chart of these birds. An excellent chart of this kind showing nineteen of the most likeable kinds of parakeets is published at Bird Haven, Reseda, California. See Bibliography, page 111.

Care of Parrots

Cages for parrots should be much larger and roomier than for other birds. They should contain plenty of perches of good hard wood and should be large enough to fit the feet of the birds comfortably. The ends of the perches should be covered with metal for about an inch or so, to prevent the birds whittling the end of the wood with their beaks. Of course, you can keep your parrot outside of a cage on a stand, the bird being tethered to the stand with a fine lightweight, perfectly smooth chain, but it is more of a nuisance to care for a bird in this way than when it is comfortable in its own cage. Cover the floor of the cage with good clean grit; that is, sprinkle it thickly over the tray in the bottom of the cage.

Parrots seem to tame more easily if confined in a cage with only one side of bars, and the other three sides solid. This sort of a cage also protects them effectively from drafts.

Be sure that the cages—bottoms, sides and all—are thoroughly cleaned and scrubbed; scrub the perches especially, at least once a week, or oftener, if your bird's habits are untidy.

Some people introduce twigs of trees into the cage. These are excellent, as they give the birds perches with different shapes and sizes of footholds, and also provide them with plenty of material to whittle with their beaks; if you wish your parrots to be very happy give them plenty of such whittling material. If such perches are plentiful the birds will not whittle the unavoidable woodwork of their cage.

The water baths should be shallow pans; these are simple and easily cleaned. Avoid all kinds of baths or similar devices that possess odd corners and angles; the simple things are best. It would be excellent if you can arrange to have a tiny streamlet of water in a little shallow trough running through the cage. Near the drinking fountain or streamlet, or whatever your source of water is, keep a block or two of partially decayed hard wood, or perhaps some irregular pine wood, not decayed; for these birds seem to need a certain amount of wood fibre as well as the grit in the digestive tract. Not only this, but they need to keep their bills in good repair by whittling, as we have said. But the perch-wood and twigs are not to be placed too near the drinking source.

It is usually an advantage to keep two birds rather than one, for these parrots and their kind seem to enjoy companionship, and indeed seem to crave it, more than do the smaller songbirds. If the species you have are of two different sorts, and of different sizes, then it is well not to keep them in one cage, but in two cages placed close beside each other.

Sometimes, during a warm summer rain, take the bottom off the cage and let the cage sit on the warm wet grass, and allow the bird to be in the warm gentle rain for a while. It will show pleasure in being so rained upon, and will roll about in the warm wet grass and get a good bath in this way.

Feeding

In the matter of feeding, parrots may be grouped into two categories; the lories and lorikeets, or the brushy-tongued parrots, and the other parrots, which we may call the smooth-tongued parrots. The first group, the lories and their kin, should be fed with soft foods. Some of the best of these are: fresh fruits such as bananas, apples, grapes, peaches, strawberries, and the like—avocados if you can afford them, but in very small quantities—melon; a bit of yellow tomato now and then; also whole-wheat bread moistened with scalded or boiled milk; figs and dates, well softened with hot water or hot milk; corn-meal mush, boiled rice, etc., are also good variations in the menu. If seeds are given to the members of this group they should be the smaller seeds, such as hemp, millet, and the ordinary canary seed, but should be well softened with hot water. Be sure also to give the birds some animal food in the form of meal worms, ant eggs, and any large soft-bodied insects you are able to capture. Crickets and grasshoppers are relished, but do not give these birds any of the very hard-shelled beetles.

The so-called smooth-tongued parrots, such as the conures, cockatoos, and larger parrots like the Gray Parrot, and the Amazons, etc., are to be fed chiefly on hard dry seeds. Suggestions for such foods are: sunflower seed, kaffir corn, corn, wheat, buckwheat, oats, and some of the smaller seeds such as the canary seed, millet and hemp, though these should be used but sparingly. Of course, the smaller the bird the smaller the seeds. Lovebirds like best the smaller seeds, and the big parrots like best the sunflower seeds, as might be expected.

Once in a while you may wish to give your birds a little special "party." For this you might use, sparingly, and not too often such tidbits as crackers, dry toast, zweiback, mashed or just plain boiled potato, sweet or white; and some of the common mixed nuts purchased at a candy store: peanuts, cashews, Brazil nuts, hazel nuts, pecans, walnuts, and the like. Coconut meat is also permissible, but should be fed only very sparingly.

Of course, green leafy foods are always to be provided, and are as necessary in the diet of these birds as in our own. Among the best are: chickweed, dandelion, soft grass, or any of the wild leafy foods except those known to be poisonous to humans. Water cress is excellent, as are also spinach, beet tops, etc. Parrots love to pull flowers to pieces and eat what they like, and almost any blossom can be fed with impunity. Also give them the seed-heads of almost any of the common roadside and field weeds. Lettuce and cabbage are recommended only after the leaves have been wilted, and parsley seems to be undesirable, though I have known birds to eat it with no ill effects. Smooth-tongued parrots should avoid bread-and-milk, sweets of any kind, and meat. These foods usually cause indigestion, and will result in the birds seeking relief by feather-pulling. Nor should the birds be fed with oranges, or other acid fruits.

Grit, of course, is a necessity for these birds as well as for others. Use a large sharp coarse sand, with which has been mixed some coarse salt, and clam or oyster shell, and some charcoal.

Breeding Parrots

This is so special a subject that the beginner had best procure promptly a good parrot breeding book; it will not do to enter into the breeding of any birds in an amateur fashion. See page 48.

Teaching Parrots to Talk

Here again is a very special branch of what we may call bird pedagogy; yet the rules are simple, and anyone with a little patience and common sense can teach fairly well. A few hints may be in order. In the parrot world the male birds respond more quickly and effectively to teaching than do the females. In teaching a parrot to talk, repetition, the keystone of success, should be carried on in a certain way. The bird should be placed in a room all by itself. It should be a warm room, a room not too brightly lighted, and, most important of all, a quiet room. The teacher is hidden behind a screen, and from this point repeats the sounds which he desires the bird to repeat. These sounds may be words, or whistles, musical sounds, etc. Some teachers recommend putting the bird in a room which is darkened, but not to pitch blackness, however. Of course, it is not wholly necessary to hide oneself while teaching your bird to talk. Usually it is more interesting to the teacher, and perhaps to the bird, to be face to face, but the teaching process will take longer under these conditions. The bird's attention is distracted by what it sees, and the object of the teaching is to have the bird's attention directed to but one thing at a time.

Naturally, young birds are more teachable than old birds, and birds that have been bred and reared in captivity are more teachable than an adult wild trapped bird.

Do not allow anyone to tease your parrot. Under the constant annoyance of teasing, your pet will develop into a screamer, and this will effectually block any success in teaching it to talk or sing or whistle.

Remember that a parrot cannot put words together to make a sentence. You may teach it the words: "hat," "your," "go," and "get," but it would never say, "Go get your hat," unless you teach it this complicated series of sounds as a single whole, like "Gogetyourhat." You may ask your pet a question, and always supply an answer to it. If you are skillful, you can teach him the answer, and bring this forth whenever you put the question, without the bird's learning to say the question. There are endless delights in this department of bird teaching, as you will learn the longer you are associated with your feathery pet.

For details in training parrots, budgerigars and like birds to talk, consult the Bibliography, page 111.

Feeding Parakeets

Parakeets must not be fed on ordinary "bird seed." They require a special diet, different from such smaller cage birds as the canaries. A good food mixture is made as follows: large red millet, one part; large yellow millet, two parts; two or three parts best plain canary seed and two parts of small sunflower seed. To this might be added one part of persicaria seed. Special Budgerigar seed rations are put up in boxes for convenience, but it is always more interesting to a bird keeper to make his own mixtures.

Green leafy foods may be fed to parakeets as well as to the smaller cage birds, but some do not recommend lettuce, or advise using it very sparingly. Clover and alfalfa are excellent green foods, as is also water cress. Spinach, Swiss chard, radish tops, and the like, are also good. Do not leave a lot of green food, or any soft vegetable food in the cage long enough to grow moldy or soft and mushy; feed it fresh and crisp each day; at about two or three-day intervals. Be sure that it is thoroughly washed and thoroughly dried.

Cuttlebone should be placed in the cage and a supply always kept there. Also provide the birds with plenty of eggshell. This will make their own eggshells firm and hard.

Purchase from your bird dealer a supply of some good brand of mineral grit; don't provide your birds merely with coarse sand, or clean bird grit.

Pure water is essential; clean the cups daily, see that the water is clear and clean at all times. The best sort of drinking fountain for these birds is the ordinary chicken drinking fountain, made of crockery; the kind that consists of a tall container which lets down the water into a saucer as the birds drink. Or one may make a homemade apparatus, by means of which water slowly drops from an elevated container into a shallow saucer below. The birds seem to enjoy this dripping water. The water drops should come very slowly, so that evaporation, plus the drinking of the birds, keeps it from running all over the bottom of the cage. A little experimenting will show you just how this is to be regulated.

If you wish your birds to nest, supply them with all sorts of coarse grass stems: straw, raffia, coarse excelsior, and the like; but do not give them long pieces of anything which they might get twisted around their legs or necks. For details of the breeding of parakeets, consult the Bibliography, page 111.

Psittacosis, or Parrot Fever

The disease sometimes occurring in parrots, and some years ago thought to be carried exclusively by birds of this family, and known as Psittacosis, or Parrot Fever, is now known to occur in, and to be transmitted by, many other sorts of birds. Canaries and other species of birds are subject to it. It is caused by an ultra-microscopic organism known as a filterable virus. These viruses are perhaps the smallest of living organisms, and there is still some doubt as to their exact position between the animate and the inanimate world. They are known as filterable viruses because they are able to pass through the excessively fine pores of a porcelain filter. The Psitticosis virus is easily transmissible from the birds to man—a faculty it shares with most viruses, such as the viruses of smallpox, infantile paralysis, measles, mumps, common colds and others.

Even without actually handling infected birds, it is possible to contract the fever, for it is often transmitted by the discharges of the birds, or by their feathers, or by the fine dust floating from the cages. Even the cages in which diseased birds were formerly housed may be an effective carrier of the viruses. The incubation period of the disease—that is, the time when the clinical symptoms develop enough to be recognizable—is usually from a week to two weeks in humans, and the symptoms are much like those of influenza or paratyphoid. Parrots and other birds suspected of carrying this disease should be taken to a veterinarian, to be disposed of at his discretion; and the person who has contracted the disease should see his doctor without delay.

Of the more than five hundred cases reported from the United States and Canada, a large proportion were traced to birds other than members of the parrot group. Some of the recently discovered antibiotics have proved effective in the treatment of the disease, and it is now regarded with less apprehension than formerly, though it still is a serious malady.

If you wish to read further about the disease, its history, diagnosis and treatment, consult: Mandell and Jordan, American Journal of Hygiene, 1952, volume 55, pages 230 to 238; Hull, *Diseases Transmitted from Animals to Man,* 3rd edition, 1947; C. C. Thomas, Springfield, Ill.; also Rivers, T. M. and Others, *Viral and Rickettsial Infections of Man,* 1948, National Foundation for Infantile Paralysis, Inc., published by J. B. Lippincott, New York.

The Reproductive Systems of the Cock and Hen

Reproductive System of the Cock

Within the two testes of the cock-bird are produced the sperms for the fertilizing of the female's eggs. The testes of birds are entirely internal, and are located against the dorsal wall of the coelom. They discharge their seminal products through two long tubes, called *vasa deferentia,* into the cloaca directly. There is usually no penis. The lower ends of the *vasa deferentia* are sometimes slightly expanded to form two thin-walled sacs for the temporary storage of the seminal products before copulation. In most cases the sperms from the cloaca of the male are transferred to the cloaca of the female by a close application of the one orifice against the other. The cloacal opening of the male lies in a slightly elevated papilla, which is slightly directed backwards, and is not prominent except during the mating season, when it projects somewhat more conspicuously.

Reproductive System of the Hen

The right ovary and oviduct of birds are usually vestigial, but from the left ovary, where the ova are produced, there descends a long coiled tube, the oviduct, which opens, like the vas deferns of the male, into the cloaca. The upper end of the oviduct spreads out into a funnel, or trumpet, to catch the ova as they are extruded from the ovary, for strange as it may seem, there is no direct connection here. The ova break out of the ovary, and are caught by ciliary action, and swept into the opening of the oviduct. Several things may happen if the ova fail to be captured by the funnel of the oviduct and go astray in the body-cavity. They may cause very serious, often fatal, disturbances in the bird. They may, however, be rapidly disintegrated, and absorbed into the blood capillaries of the walls of the peritoneum; or they may be caught and walled-off by the peritoneum, and held there until subsequent slow absorption takes place.

The insemination, or introduction of the sperms into the cloaca of the hen, is followed by the rapid ascent of the motile spermatozoa up through the oviduct, to the top or funnel of the same, in which region their penetration into the ova takes place. Insemination does not always, therefore, mean successful fertilization, though it normally follows.

As the ovum descends through the oviduct, it receives its coating of albumen (white) and later its deposit of membrane, shell, and pigments, if any. All this time, of course, the original ovum has been dividing rapidly; the cells dividing by twos—two, four, eight, sixteen, thirty-two, etc.—until finally the blastoderm begins to envelope the yolk part of the ovum, and form the little embryo bird lying on it, and drawing its nourishment for growth from the yellow yolk or food material of the embryo. All this goes on within the jelly-like albumen, and then later within the albumen and the shell.

Usually the hen has no trouble in extruding, or laying, her eggs, but if the walls of the cloaca or adjoining region become constricted, or if for any

REPRODUCTIVE SYSTEMS OF THE COCK AND HEN

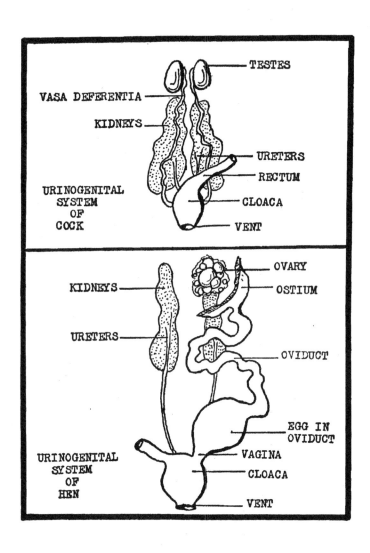

reason the egg is difficult to release, then the condition called egg-binding has supervened, and remedies must be given in the bird's aid. For these, see page 34.

The Digestive System of Birds

Digestion, usually beginning at once in the mouth of most vertebrate animals, with the mixing of the saliva with the food, is in birds reduced to a minimum. Songbirds possess few and small glands; in some species they are virtually absent. Small birds seize and bolt their food at once, and it passes down the esophagus into an expanded portion of the esophageal tube, a portion known as the crop. In the seed-eating birds, such as the canaries and their kind, the crop is well developed, and the seeds are swallowed down into it, some cracked, others bolted whole. In the crop this mass is stored, mixed with mucus from the glands along the walls.

From the crop, the food mass is urged by constrictions of muscles along the walls into the first portion of the bird's stomach, known as the *proventriculus;* for the birds really possess two stomachs. It is in the *proventriculus* that the first of the digestive juices are poured over the food, juices that are secreted by minute glands in the *proventriculus* walls, these glands being arranged either in patches, or more usually in long bands.

After the food mass has been thoroughly mixed with digestive juices, it is squeezed into the second part of the bird's stomach, the gizzard. This organ is thick, heavy, with strong muscular walls; no doubt, you are familiar with the gizzard of a stewed chicken, and know how very thick and strong and compact are the heavy gray muscles that compose it. The gizzard powerfully compresses, squeezes and grinds up the food, and is aided in this work by the grit which the bird has swallowed, the grit acting like so many tiny little millstones for pulverizing the food mass. Since the birds have no teeth it is really within the muscular gizzard that the food is finally masticated, we might say.

The food mass, mixed with digestive juices, and now thoroughly ground up, resembles a thick cream soup; and such it really is, a highly nourishing mixture, which the bird now proceeds to absorb into its blood vessels. Up to this point, no food has entered the bird's body economy; it has only been slowly moved through a canal, being prepared as it went, for taking into the real body, which is, of course, the living cells of the bird. It is in the intestine of the bird that the absorption of the liquid food takes place. For no food in a solid state can get into the bird's blood stream; it must first be liquified, that is to say, digested.

The intestine of birds varies greatly in length; the ostrich, for example possesses forty-six feet of intestine; the humming-bird only two inches; the smaller songbirds have intestines of varying lengths, but usually not much longer than their bodies. The intestine is very much coiled, and into its upper part, or duodenum, there open the digestive glands of the pancreas, liver and the minute intestinal glands which line its walls.

The food-soup, as we may truly call it, is now ready. It has been mixed with mucus, *proventriculus* juices, ground up to a paste in the gizzard, and now finally mixed with pancreatic juice, bile (from the liver), and intestinal juice (from the microscopic intestinal glands of the duodenum). As it goes rapidly (in birds it is very rapid) down the course of the rest of the intestine, below the duodenum, it is absorbed

THE DIGESTIVE SYSTEM OF BIRDS

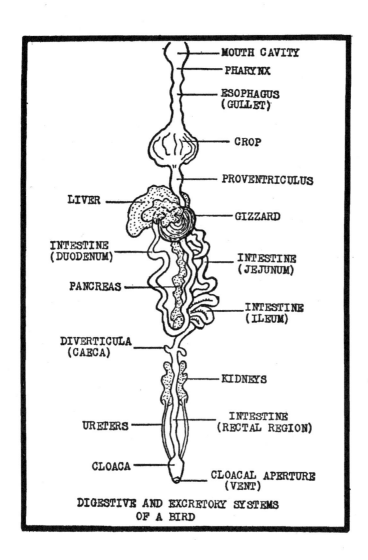

DIGESTIVE AND EXCRETORY SYSTEMS OF A BIRD

into the blood vessels, and carried swiftly to all parts of the body, mingled with the blood itself, in order to nourish the billions of cells of the bird's muscles, bones, brain, skin, connective and other tissues.

Digestion and absorption in the small song birds is very complete and perfect, as may be inferred from the extreme shortness of the large intestine and rectum, which contain very little undigested material.

Birds possess two kidneys, but no bladder, and the liquid waste filtered from the blood by the kidneys is conducted by tubes directly into the cloaca, or hindmost part of the intestine, and is voided together with the undigested substances *(feces)*. The *feces* of the normally healthy cage bird are semi-solid, and their condition is often a valuable index of the state of health of the bird.

The Respiratory System of Birds

The respiration of birds is in some respects unique. The lungs are relatively small, and unlike those of mammals, especially man, are only very slightly distensible; the bird cannot protrude its chest and lower its diaphragm, and puff itself out, so to speak, and, as we do, take a deep breath. To compensate for this, the respiration of birds is much more rapid than ours, and, moreover, is assisted by the strokes of the wing in flying. Hence cage birds which have plenty of room to exercise their wings have increased powers of respiration thereby. Expiration is the active part of the bird's respiratory movements, not inspiration, as in ours. The diagram (page 85) shows the principal structures in the respiratory system of a small songbird. It will be seen that the larynx, the voice-box in humans, has no vocal cords in the birds, and hence is not a voice-box for them. The vocal cords in birds, from whence the song proceeds, are situated in a structure known as the syrinx, to be found at the junction of the trachea or windpipe, and the two bronchi.

The air-sac system, additional respiratory chambers and tubes, is peculiar to birds, and to some reptiles, and is one of the many indications of the close affinity and remote ancestral relationship of these two groups. The air-sacs and their tubules conduct air from the lungs and trachea to many remote parts of the body. Some of the long thin sacs or tubes even pierce the bones, as is shown in our diagram. The inner walls of the sacs are ciliated, but they are very poorly supplied with blood capillaries, hence do not function in respiration as lungs do. They greatly increase the amount of air which the bird has stored up in the system, and this important extra supply is used in many ways; in songbirds chiefly as supplying a large volume used in vigorous and protracted song. It is somewhat like the supply of air in the bellows or air chamber of a pipe organ. Another use of this large volume of stored air is to furnish a fresh supply upon expiration. The bird, therefore, has a double tide or flow of oxygenated air into the lungs; one flow upon inspiration, another flow upon expiration. No other animal has such an advantage. Still another function of the air-sacs is to provide large surfaces for internal perspiration, for birds have no external skin glands for this purpose. The inner surfaces of the sacs therefore, in this process of evaporation, help control the heat of the bird's body. Large amounts of water are got rid of in this way. You will remember that birds drink large quantities of water; yet they do not urinate, and there is not much water in their *feces*. Still another use of the air-sacs, and some think an important one, is to provide cushions for the easy movements of the visceral organs in flight, and in the many other violent activities of the bird.

Since the lungs of a bird are scarcely distensible, a bird must breathe, that is inspire and expire very rapidly, and this it does at the surprising rate of some twenty to sixty times a minute. We humans breathe at the rate of about thirteen to sixteen times a minute.

THE RESPIRATORY SYSTEM OF BIRDS

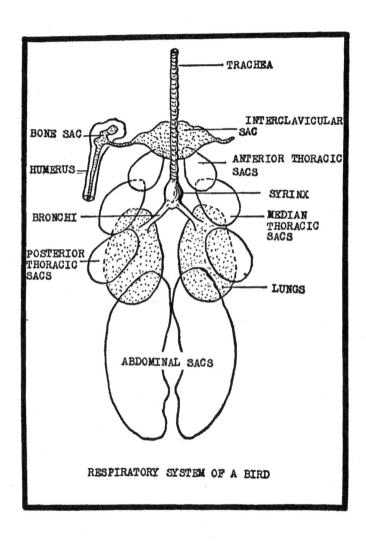

RESPIRATORY SYSTEM OF A BIRD

The Circulatory System of Birds

The circulation of blood in the body of a bird is extremely rapid. The heart, with its four chambers almost exactly like our own, is perhaps the most efficient little pump known in the entire animal world. It beats over a hundred times a minute when the bird is at rest, but with activity this rate becomes doubled; and if the bird is highly disturbed or frightened, and struggles about madly, the heart may beat so fast as to make the flutters of its pulsations too rapid to be counted.

The normal pulsations of a small bird's heart sends the blood squirting in lightning-like jets throughout all the arteries, arterioles, and capillaries of the body; whence it returns to the heart through the venules and veins. It is necessary for this to be so, for you remember the bird's respiration rate is very rapid also, and oxygen must be carried to the billions of cells of the bird's body, and their waste products removed and carried away. Birds' temperatures are very high, too, some 112 degrees Fahrenheit more or less, and usually more!

This matter of the body temperature of birds is a most surprising thing. It is far higher than ours, of course, ours being a mere 98.7 degrees Fahrenheit or so. Even with this very moderate heat in our furnaces, we must keep going down our gullets a surprising amount of food; it is even more essential for the birds to keep a larger quantity going down theirs. The temperature of a bird incubating her eggs, for

THE CIRCULATORY SYSTEM OF BIRDS 87

example, is somewhere in the neighborhood of 107 degrees; and when the bird is active the temperature rises much above this.

It might be interesting to compare the high body temperature of cage birds with the temperatures of some of our common wild birds. These are roughly in degrees Fahrenheit:

>   Mourning Dove 109
>   Ruby-Throated Hummingbird 109
>   Downy Woodpecker 108
>   Red-Bellied Woodpecker 110
>   Bluebird 110
>   Crested Flycatcher 111
>   Robin 113

Variations of these temperatures within ten degrees are not unusual at different hours of the day and under different conditions of bodily activity. The little House Wren, for example, may show a body temperature of 116 degrees.

Our cage birds are kept warm and comfortable, and the temperature of their bodies does not vary a great deal, except under high excitement, to which, of course, they never should be subjected.

It is different with our wild native birds. The body temperature of the next spring Bluebird you see in your garden, perhaps on a raw and freezing day in March, will be probably not far from 110 degrees. But what about the tiny little Chickadees of our northern forests and mountains? I have watched flocks of these hardy and cheerful little birds in our northern New England mountains looking for small hibernating insects, calling to each other, each call being accompanied by tiny puffs of steam from their little beaks; and all the while a brisk breeze was blowing, and the thermometer stood at thirty degrees below zero! Yet here were these diminutive little midgets, each one with a body, when denuded of its feathers, not much bigger than the first joint of one's thumb, maintaining a constant body heat well over one hundred degrees! Think of what this means in terms of body activity and physiology: the rapid inrush and outrush of air between the outside and the almost microscopic lungs; the mad triphammer pumping of the tiny pea-sized heart; the swift spurt and surge of the fine streamlets of blood loaded with oxygen and food and waste materials as well, as the streams race at top speed throughout the thousands upon thousands of fine blood vessels—even out into those fine wire-like toes—out and back, out and back, before you can say Jack Robinson! It is truly a matter of paralyzing wonderment that so minute a speck of flesh and blood can keep its fierce flush of hot life going underneath the relatively thin blanket of feathers, in the very teeth of such bitter sub-zero temperatures. So the next time you look at your own pet bird, for instance, just think what a fiery little furnace in feathers it is.

A Word About Out-of-Door Aviaries

Although the present book deals with the smaller birds and with home cage birds, suitable for the home or small apartment, or even for one room, yet a word about the practice of keeping birds out-of-doors seems needed to make the book more complete. For when you begin with a bird in a cage in a room, very often your interests progressively widen, and you begin to think of keeping a pair or two of birds in a sun porch. Then you say, why not have a little separate house for them out in the yard, and perhaps buy a few more pairs, or have some different species.

This means that you are beginning to think in terms of an out-of-door aviary. Of course, there are indoor aviaries, but we are thinking now of the one out-of-doors. In general, an aviary is maintained in a different way from a cage, whether it is indoor or out-door.

If your aviary is merely another house, or large room, with a row of cages along one or two sides, then your problem is merely the problem of one cage, multiplied by the number of cages you keep. But if you intend to erect a large cage, say one 12 feet square, out-of-doors, then you must see to it that three sides are of good thick wood, as an insulation against the cold. One side may be of wire. The bottom should be of concrete, and the wire on the front of the cage should be securely fastened to the concrete base in such a way that rats and mice, squirrels, skunks, and weasels, and the like, cannot find entrance. Around the other three sides, near the bottom, run the wire up as a sort of apron several feet high (or use sheet metal), so that here too, the vermin cannot find an entrance.

The door by which you enter the aviary yourself must also be similarly protected. Make your aviary high enough so that your birds will feel they have plenty of flying space; birds will not roost if they find that the roof is too near the floor. Some aviarists make the sleeping or roosting portion of the aviary at the back a few feet higher than the flying part of the little building, that is the part at the front where the single wire-side is. The perches should be placed up high, and this portion of the building should be so made that it is possible to close it off from the flying part in severe weather. Hardy birds should be allowed to fly freely, and to be in the open as much as possible even in the worst of weather; otherwise they gradually become inactive, put on weight, acquire constipation, and get fat and lazy, and acquire ailments.

The aviary should be situated in a protected spot, and be so placed that the wire-side of the building faces south or south-east. The back of the building, where the roosting perches are, should be protected from the rays of the sun in summer by over-arching trees or by thick running vines. This keeps the roosting part of the building from becoming too hot for roosting. The leaves will fall off as winter comes on, and return in the spring, and thus make an automatic heat-check over your aviary which needs no attention on your part to operate. At the front of your aviary, where the wire is, provide some means of keeping a part of the interior in the shade during the hot months. Birds love to sit in the sun, but again, also like to find agreeable shade.

The wire used on the front of the building should not be so thick and close-meshed as to prevent good

A WORD ABOUT OUT-OF-DOOR AVIARIES

clear views of the interior. I have seen such close-meshed wire used on aviaries as to make it impossible to see the birds inside unless one pressed one's face against the wire and then made a shade of one's hand. Even then the view was very unsatisfactory. The wire may be covered with a bitumen paint, or a sort of black varnish which comes especially for screens. It is important to keep this wire a dead black, as it reflects very little light and makes an interior view very easy indeed. The birds will not fly against it, even if it seems almost invisible from the outside. They soon learn that there is something there. It is only perfectly clean, clear glass that puzzles birds; they never seem to get used to it or understand it. It is so utterly different from anything they encounter in their ordinary habitats; or that their ancestors had encountered generations before. Use an old pair of gardening shears for cutting the wire, and when you attach it do not use nails bent over, nor yet staples, but put it on with laths, which makes a much neater bit of work and is easier to tighten.

When you paint the aviary look well to the kind of paint. If you are housing birds of the parrot tribe, which are likely to bite and whittle the wood with their beaks, do not use a lead paint, which is very injurious to birds. Even when a lead-base paint is used for other birds the aviary must be allowed to dry out for a week or so, before the birds are introduced, until all the odor of the paint has wholly disappeared.

Some persons make an aviary in the corner or angle of their homes; this is excellent in many ways. It gives through one, or perhaps two windows, a fine view of the birds from indoors; it permits feeding in winter without going out-of-doors, and, best of all, provides two sides of the aviary with warm walls for the winter. One side of this should be furnished with perches, and perhaps a little inside roof put up, with considerable overhang, under which the birds on their elevated perches feel snug and secure for the night.

Moveable aviaries are often made of light materials, the floor being of metal, with a metal or wire apron all around to exclude predators at night. This, if it be made about eight feet square, can easily be moved by two men from one part of the garden to another, according to the season, or it can be put on a flat truck and moved anywhere you wish. In fact you might build up a business of making portable aviaries!

The floor of the aviary should always be covered with clean washed sand, or with sawdust, to the depth of at least an inch. Beach sand is good for this purpose, but it should be coarse sand, not the very fine sand that one sometimes sees. If sawdust is used see that it is clean; wash it in hot water, then let it dry out before putting it on the floor. Both the sand and the sawdust should be renewed frequently.

Small evergreen trees in pots may be placed around the walls inside the aviary, and a large dead limb (or small tree) with many convenient branches may be erected in the middle. On the side walls other twigs, or peg perches may be fastened.

If your aviary contains finches and other seed eaters, then you should attach self-feeding seed hoppers on the wall, and also offer the drinking water in a self-supplying bird fountain. Both of these can be had in any pet shop, or having seen several patterns you can then go home and make your own. Making devices for your aviary is one of the great pleasures of bird keeping.

When you feed green leafy foods, or vegetables or fruits, or mush or egg food, or any other soft food, do so on little shelves attached to the walls. Keep the floor from becoming messed up as far as you can.

In putting up furniture in your aviary such as little

A WORD ABOUT OUT-OF-DOOR AVIARIES 93

trees, branches, shelves, fountains, mechanical feeders, nesting boxes (at the proper seasons), be sure that you make no little corners and crevices and places where birds are apt to become trapped.

The bath should be a large pan or earthenware dish, very shallow, the water not more than an inch and a half deep (for the finches and smaller birds, that is), and may be placed on the floor of the cage. It should not be left there permanently, say some; others say it may be left. Whatever rule you follow, see to it that no foul water is allowed to accumulate.

If you live in a neighborhood where cats may be a problem, then it is best to make the open front of your aviary of a double wall of wire, with a space of about five inches between, to prevent the cats from climbing up and coming too near the birds and frightening them.

Some fanciers provide two small doors for their aviaries, the first one opening into a little antechamber, the second one into the cage room itself. When entering, the outer door is closed before the inner one is opened. I have known many a bird to slip out and escape from an out-of-door aviary that had only one door.

In these large aviaries there is always a considerable amount of teasing, pestering and actual fighting among the birds, since the birds in such an enclosure court and mate quite at random. A great deal of this can be prevented by regulating the numbers of the sexes, so that the females outnumber the males by two to one.

Compartment aviaries are often used where extensive and controlled breeding is going on. But each compartment should be not less than three feet wide by four feet high. This, I know, will seem too large to many readers, but I am strongly of the opinion that birds do best when they are not in the least crowded.

If you have the space for an out-door aviary this amount of room will not be difficult to provide.

To give the reader a general idea of what birds can be successfully grouped together in a typical outdoor aviary, the following rules are given, which, however, must be modified according to your specific needs and wishes and limitations. In all these groups you must watch your birds carefully after the grouping, and remove at once the unamiable members of your close community. A little "practice will make perfect" here.

I. NON-BREEDING GROUPS

The following birds are placed together for their general decorative effect and interest of habits, etc., but not for mating and breeding.

1. The larger thrushes, Mynahs, Starlings, Tanagers, Bulbuls (larger species) and Jays.
2. Pekin Robin (Chinese Nightingale, or Japanese Nightingale), Sibias, Larks, small Bulbuls.
3. Grass Finches, Waxbills, Chinese or Button Quails, Canaries, Zebra Finches.
4. Weaver Birds, Chinese Robins (Japanese Nightingales), small Tanagers, small Bulbuls.

II. MATING AND BREEDING GROUPS

1. One pair of each of the following: Diamond Doves, Cordon Bleus, Masked Grassfinches, Gouldian Finches, Bicheno or Ringed Finches.
2. One pair of each of the following: Diamond Doves, Silverbills, Rufous-Tailed Grassfinches, Chestnut-Breasted Finches, Gray or Singing Finches.
3. One pair of each of the following: Diamond Doves, Cordon Bleus, Blue-Breasted Waxbills, Fire Finches, Orange-Cheeked Gray Waxbills, Golden-Breasted Waxbills.

A WORD ABOUT OUT-OF-DOOR AVIARIES

4. One pair of each of the following: Senegal Doves, Magpie Mannikins, White Java Sparrows, Pileated Finches.

5. One pair of each of the following: Cockatiels, Crested Doves, California Quails, Saffron Finches, Java Sparrows.

6. One pair of each of the following: Cape or Tambourine or Half-Collared or Passerine Doves, Chinese Painted Quails, Goldfinches, any small species of the Serin Finches, Bronze Mannikins, Silverbills, Rufous-Backed Mannikins, Spice Mannikins.

Since the writer has had no experience in the breeding of these birds, it should be noted that the above suggested breeding groupings has been compiled from Luke and Silver's splendid book, *Aviaries, Birdrooms and Cages,* London, November, 1950, 5th edition.

The Training of Cage Birds

The training of birds involves first of all the question: for what do I wish to train my bird? If the bird is a parrot or a parakeet, or a bird of this group, then the training is usually a course of talking lessons, first of all. This is a broad subject, and we cannot treat of it here. However we can refer you to three excellent books on the subject. They are:—(1) *Talking Budgerigars and How to Train Them,* by Andrew Wilson. Dorset House, Stamford Street, London, England. (2) *Teaching the Budgerigar to Talk,* by M. L. and F. Flowers. Bird Haven, Reseda, California. (3) *Parrots and Other Talking Birds,* by C. N. Page. Published by the author, Des Moines, Iowa.

If you wish to train birds to perform any special antics, or for exhibition purposes—where display and the competition for prizes is the object—then you are entering the professional field, for display and the securing of prizes usually means that you wish to use these recognitions to advertise and sell the progeny of your breeding stock, or sell especially trained birds. If you wish merely to train your bird to sing in certain ways, or to be at home as it flies freely about the room, or to sit on your finger or head, or to take food from your hand or lips, etc., there are a host of suggestions for you to wade through, in these books that are now suggested:

(1) *Exhibition Budgerigars,* by M. D. S. Armour. Dorset House, Stamford Street, London, England. (2)

THE TRAINING OF CAGE BIRDS

Guide to Canary Breeding and Exhibiting, by W. E. Brooks. Dorset House, Stamford Street, London, England. (3) *Revised Encyclopaedia of Cage Birds, Canaries, Parakeets, Finches, Mules and Hybrids,* by H. and N. M. Fogg. Audubon Publishing Company, Louisville, Kentucky. (4) *The Roller Canary, All About Its Song and Training,* by H. W. Gutierrez. Dorset House, Stamford Street, London, England. (5) *Norwich Canaries, Their Breeding, Management, and Exhibiting,* by C. A. House. Dorset House, Stamford Street, London, England. (6) "My Experiences with Cockatiels," by E. L. Moon. *All Pets Magazine,* Fond du Lac, Wisconsin. (7) *The Cult of the Budgerigar,* by W. Watmough. Dorset House, Stamford Street, London, England. (8) *Questions Answered About Cage Birds,* by Andrew Dick. Jordan and Sons, London, England.

For the training of any bird to come to the hand, or to sing after hearing notes on a piano, flute, or violin, or from simple whistling; or to train a bird to become accustomed to the freedom of a room while its cage is being cleaned, or to perform any small amusing tricks—all that is necessary is patience, coaxing, repetition, and always, at the successful close of any lesson, rewarding the little pet with some especially dainty food which it is not in the habit of receiving regularly. Cage birds of any kind are especially sensitive creatures, much more so than cats, dogs, or other mammal pets, and must be treated in such a way during the course of any training as not to upset them and make them nervous. The symptoms of such nervousness will at once be recognized by any pet-loving person. At such times, and perhaps always after a long lesson, and when the bird has been rewarded with the especial tidbits reserved for the occasion, it should be placed back in its cage; and the cage partially covered for a time to keep it warm and a bit dusky within and to give the bird a chance to relax for a time.

However one must be careful about this matter of covering a bird in a cage. Some birds welcome the utter privacy and dim light that this covering gives, whereas other birds are made extremely fidgety by such treatment. If your bird shows plainly that it dislikes being covered, then remove the cage, if you notice that a lesson has made the bird fidgety, to a quiet room, for a time, especially to a room where the bird will have a little extra warmth. If it is left here for half an hour or so, the chances are that it will cuddle itself into a ball of feathers on its perch and take a nap. It is never wise to give a bird any sort of sedative, except under the advice of a veterinarian. Warmth and quiet are the best natural pacifiers for birds who are not in need of special medical attention.

The following pages show some of the most popular of the canaries, smaller finches, and others; as well as some of the parakeets, love birds, and parrots; those which, it has been found, thrive best under home domestication.

For extended descriptions of these birds, and for colored illustrations of these, and many others, one should consult the special books listed in the Bibliography.

Bird Haven, at Reseda, California, publishes splendid color charts (without text) of scores of the common canaries and other finches, as well as of smaller birds, and of the parrots, parakeets, love birds, conures, and the like. Address: *Bird Haven, Reseda, California.*

PLATE I

PLATE II

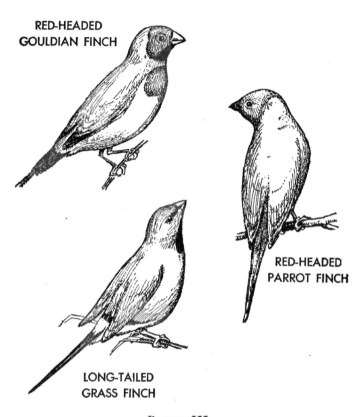

PLATE III

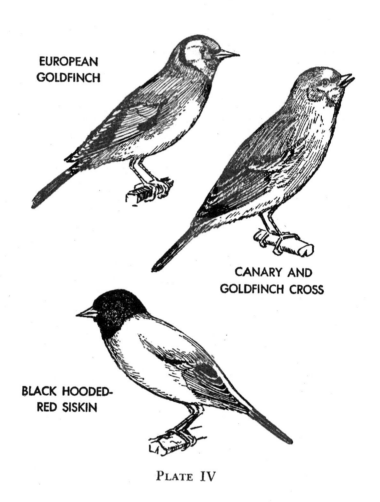

Plate IV

PLATE V

PLATE VI

PLATE VII

RED-HEADED CONURE

Plate VIII

**BLUE-FRONTED
AMAZON PARROT**

Plate IX

PANAMA PARROT

PLATE X

MEXICAN DOUBLE
YELLOW-HEADED PARROT

Plate XI

DWARF PARROT

Plate XII

Bibliography

Helpful Books and Periodicals Devoted to Cage Birds

I. Books

Armour, M. D. S., *Exhibition Budgerigars*, Dorset House, Stamford St., London, England.

———, *Inbreeding Budgerigars*, Dorset House, Stamford St., London, England.

"Bird," *The Canary, Its Care and Treatment*, R. T. French Co., Rochester, N. Y., 1933.

———, *All About Your Canary*, R. T. French Co., Rochester, N. Y., 1951.

"Bird Haven," *Canaries, Their Care and Breeding*, Bird Haven, Reseda, California, 1952.

———, *Aviary and Cage Birds*, Bird Haven, Reseda, California, 1952.

Bechstein, J. M., *Cage and Chamber Birds*, G. Bell and Sons, London, 1905.

Blackston, Swaysland, and Wiener, *The Illustrated Book of Canaries and Cage Birds*, Cassell and Co., London, England, 1901.

Bronson, J. L., *Parrot Family Birds*, All Pets Magazine, Fond du Lac, Wisconsin, 1951.

Brooks, W. E., *Guide to Canary Breeding and Exhibiting*, Dorset House, Stamford St., London, England, 1947.

———, *Shackleton's, The Yorkshire Canary*, Dorset House, Stamford St., London, England, 1894.

Brooks, W. E., *The Yorkshire Canary*, Dorset House, Stamford St., London, England, 1947.

Brooksbank, Alec, *Foreign Birds for Garden Aviaries*, Dorset House, Stamford St., London, England, 1949.
——, *Foreign Birds for Beginners*, Dorset House, Stamford St., London, England, 1951.
Dick, Andrew, *Questions Answered About Cage Birds*, Jordan and Sons, London, England, 1949.
Duncker, A., *Budgerigar Matings and Colour Expectations*, Dorset House, Stamford St., London, England.
Feyerabend, C., *Budgerigar Guide*, All Pets Magazine, Fond du Lac, Wisconsin.
——, *Diseases of Budgerigars*, All Pets Magazine, Fond du Lac, Wisconsin.
——, *Modern Feeding of Budgerigars*, All Pets Magazine, Fond du Lac, Wisconsin.
——, *The Budgerigar or Shell Parakeet as a Talker*, All Pets Magazine, Fond du Lac, Wisconsin.
——, *The Talking Budgie*, All Pets Magazine, Fond du Lac, Wisconsin.
Flowers, M. L., and F., *Parakeets, Their Care and Breeding*, Bird Haven, Reseda, California.
——, *Finches, Their Care and Breeding*, Bird Haven, Reseda, California.
——, *Teaching the Budgerigar to Talk*, Bird Haven, Reseda, California, 1950.
Fogg, H., and N. M., *Revised Encyclopaedia of Cage Birds, Canaries, Parakeets, Finches, Mules and Hybrids*, Audubon Publishing Co., Louisville, Kentucky, 1928.
Gill, A. K., *Cinnamon Inheritance in Canaries*, Dorset House, Stamford St., London, England.
——, *Canary Breeding-Room Register*, Dorset House, Stamford St., London, England.
Greene, W. T., *Parrots in Captivity*, 3 vols., George Bell and Son, Convent Garden, London, 1915.
Gutierrez, H. W., *The Roller Canary, All About Its Song and Training*, Dorset House, Stamford St., London, England.
——, *The Border Fancy Canary, Its Breeding, Rearing, and Management*, Dorset House, Stamford St., London, England.

BIBLIOGRAPHY

Hausman, Ethel H., *Beginner's Guide to Wild Flowers,* G. P. Putnam's Sons, New York, 1948 (For identifying plants producing seeds for birds).

Holden, G. H., *Canaries and Cage Birds,* published by the author, New York, 1895.

——, *The New Book of Birds,* published by the author, New York, 1919.

Houlton, C., *Cage Birds and Hybrids,* Philadelphia, Pa., 1928.

House, C. A., *Canaries, A Complete and Practical Guide,* Philadelphia, 1923.

——, *Norwich Canaries, Their Management, Breeding, and Exhibiting,* Dorset House, Stamford St., London, England.

Kirby, A., *Canary Breeding,* All Pets Magazine, Fond du Lac, Wisconsin, 1949.

Luke, L. B., and Silver, A., *Aviaries, Birdrooms, and Cages,* Dorset House, Stamford St., London, England, 1950.

Mannering, Rosslyn, *Mules and Hybrids,* All Pets Magazine, Fond du Lac, Wisconsin.

Miller, Virginia, *Your Canary,* All Pets Magazine, Fond du Lac, Wisconsin, 1951.

Morse, Richard, *Wild Plants and Seeds for Birds,* Dorset House, Stamford St., London, England, 1947 (See also Hausman, Ethel H., *Beginner's Guide to Wildflowers*).

Moon, E. L., *My Experiences with Cockatiels,* All Pets Magazine, Fond du Lac, Wisconsin.

Norman, H., *Breeding British Birds in Aviaries and Cages,* Dorset House, Stamford St., London, England.

Page, C. N., *Parrots and Other Talking Birds,* published by the author, Des Moines, Iowa, 1906.

Patterson, J., *The Border Fancy Canary,* All Pets Magagazine, Fond du Lac, Wisconsin.

Robson, J. (ed.), *The Crested Canary,* All Pets Magazine, Fond du Lac, Wisconsin.

Rogers, Cyril, *Budgerigars and How to Breed Them,* Dorset House, Stamford St., London, England.

Seth-Smith, David, *Parrakeets, A Handbook to Imported Species,* Bernard Quaritch, New Bond St., London, England, 1926.

St. John, Claude, *Bird Ailments and Accidents*, Dorset House, Stamford St., London, England, 1948.
——, *Canary Breeding for Beginners*, Dorset House, Stamford St., London, England, 1947.
Stroud, B., *Stroud's Digest of the Diseases of Birds*, All Pets Magazine, Fond du Lac, Wisconsin.
Watmough, W., *Colour Breeding in Budgerigars*, Dorset House, Stamford St., London, England.
——, *The Cult of the Budgerigar*, Dorset House, Stamford St., London, England.
——, *The Budgerigar Breeding and Show Register*, Dorset House, Stamford St., London, England.
——, *The Budgerigar Breeders' Pedigree Forms*, Dorset House, Stamford St., London, England.
Weston, Denys, *The Budgerigar in Captivity*, Dorset House, Stamford St., London, England.
Wetmore, A. T., *Canaries, Their Care and Management*, Fish and Wildlife Service, Farmer's Bulletin No. 1327, Washington, D. C., 1924.
Wilson, Andrew, *Talking Budgerigars and How to Train Them*, Dorset House, Stamford St., London, England.

II. Periodicals

The Canary Journal, Roller Fanciers' Corporation, 2002 South 17th East St., Salt Lake City, Utah.
The Canary World and Cage Bird Digest, Lecanto, Florida.
All Pets Magazine, 18 Forest Avenue, Fond du Lac, Wisconsin.
Cage Birds, Dorset House, Stamford St., London, England.

Bird Haven, at Reseda, California, is a famous headquarters for cage birds of all sorts; here are published charts, books and lists of various sorts of interest to cage bird lovers. This is also a headquarters for bird books of all publishers, both English and American.

Index

Accidents, 35-40
Africa, northern, 2
African Gray Parrot, 62
Age of birds, telling, 45
Ailments, common, 19-40
 digestive system, 22-25
 miscellaneous, 29-35
 procedure, general, 20-22
 respiratory, 25-29
Apoplexy, 31-32
Approaching bird, 7, 8
Armour, M. D. S., 96
Asia Minor, 2
Asthma, 27-28
Aviaries, out-of-door, 89-95
Azores, 2

Baldness, 38, 41
Bathing, 14-16
 out-of-door aviaries, 93
 parrots, 66
Beginner's Guide to Wildflowers, 58
Bill, overgrown, 37
Bird fever, 29
Bird Haven, Reseda, Calif., 64, 98
Bird plague, 29
Birdseed mixture, 53
Birdweed *(Stellaria media)*, 59
Bitter Dock *(Rumex obtusifolius)*, 59
Blackberry *(Rubus)*, 58

Black-Cheeked Lovebird, 104
Black Hooded Red Siskin, 102
Black Knapweed *(Centaurea nigra)*, 59
Blue-Fronted Amazon Parrot, 107
Blue Parakeets, 63-64
Body temperature, 15, 19, 86-88
Bouffleurs, Chevalierde, 5
Bound gizzard, 25
Breeding, 48-52
 parrots, 68
Broad-Leaved Dock *(Rumex obtusifolius)*, 59
Broad-Leaved Plantain *(Plantago major)*, 41, 42, 58, 60
Broken leg, 35-36
Broken wing, 36
Brooks, W. E., 97
Budgerigars, 5, 63
Budgies, 63
Bugle Bird, 4
Bullfinch, 3
Butterfly Finch, 3
Buying a bird, 6-10

Cage:
 all-metal, 12, 49
 apron, 12
 breeding, 49
 care, 11-16
 cleaning, 13, 14

INDEX

cover, 14
furniture, 11-16
parrots, 65
perches, 12
shape, 12-13
size, 12
support, 13
Canaries, 1-3, 99, 100
Canary and Goldfinch Cross, 102
Canary Islands, 1, 2, 3
Cardinals, 3
Cataract, 32
Catarrh, 27
Cheese, 54
Chickweeds (Stellaria), 58, 59
Chinese Nightingale, 4
Circulatory system, 86-88
Claws, overgrown, 37
Cockatiels, 4
Colds, common, 25-26
Color food, 55-56
Coltsfoot (Tussilago farfara), 59
Common Chickweed (Stellaria media), 59
Common colds, 25-26
Common Sow Thistle (Sonchus oleraceus), 60
Common Teasel (Dipsacus sylvestris), 60
Constipation, 24
Conures, 4
Corn Spurry (Spergula arvensis), 60
Coughwort (Tussilago farfara), 59
Crested Norwich Canary, 99
Cuban Amazon Parrot, 63
Cult of the Budgerigar, Watmough, 97
Curly Doc (Rumex crispus), 59
Cuttlebone, 14, 55, 71

Dandelion (Taxaxacum vulgare), 59
Diarrhea, 23
Dick, Andrew, 97
Digestive system, 79-82
  ailments, 22-25
Disinfectants, 13
Dislocations, 35
Doorweed (Polygonum aviculare), 59
Dutch Frill Canary, 99
Dwarf Parrot, 110
Dysentary, 23-24

Early Winter Cress (Barbarea verna), 60
Egg binding, 34-35, 50
Egg food, 52, 54-55
Eggs:
  incubation, 51
  laying, 50-51
Elba, Island of, 3
England, 3
Epilepsy, 30-31
Europe, southern, 2
European Goldfinch, 3, 11, 102
Evening Lychnis (Lychnis alba), 58
Exhibition Budgerigars, Armour, 96
Eyes, sore or inflamed, 32

Feather loss, 38
Feeding:
  molting period, 41-42
  overfeeding, 17-18
  parakeets, 71-72
  parrots, 66-68
  sick bird, 21-22
Feet, sore, 32-33
Field Mustard (Brassica arvensis), 58-59
Field Sow Thistle (Sonchus arvensis), 60
Finch mixture, 53

INDEX

Fire Finches, 3
Fischer's Lovebird, 105
Fits, 30-31
Flowers, M. L. and F., 96
Foods:
  recommended, 53-56
  wild plants as source of, 57-60
Fracture:
  leg, 36
  wing, 36
Fringillidae family, 1, 57
Fruits, 53
Fuerteventura, island of, 2
Fugg, H. and N. M., 97

General mixture, 53
Germany, 3
Goldfinches, 58
Grass Parakeets, 5
Gray Bird Louse, 39-40
Green food, 52, 53
Green Parakeets, 64
Grinsel *(Senecio vulgaris)*, 59
Grit, 56, 68
Groundsel *(Senecio vulgaris)*, 59
Guide to Canary Breeding and Exhibiting, Brooks, 97
Gutierrez, H. W., 97
Gypsy Combs *(Dipsacus sylvestris)*, 60

Hausman, E. H., *Beginner's Guide to Wildflowers*, 58
Hawthorn *(Crataegus)*, 59
Health, rules for, 17-18
Heartweed *(Polygonum persicaria)*, 59
House, C. A., 97
Huskiness, 26-27

Impaction, 25
Indigestion, 24-25

Inflamed eyes, 32
Insect food, 53

Japanese Nightingale, 4
Japanese Robin, 4
Java Sparrow, 103
Jay Thrushes, 4

Lady Gould Finch, 3
Lady's Thumb *(Polygonum)*, 58
Lancashire Coppy Canary, 100
Lanzarote, island of, 2
Leg, fracture, 35-36
Length of life, 46-47
Levaillant's Amazon Parrot, 62
Lice, 38, 39-40
Life, length, 46-47
Linnaeus, 1
Long-Tailed Grass Finch, 101
Loss of voice, 26-27
Lovebirds, 4, 5, 63, 104, 105

Macaws, 4
Madeira, 2
Marie Antoinette, 5
Masked Grass Finch, 3
Mating, 48-52
Mauve Parakeets, 64
Meadow Grass *(Poa annua)*, 59
Meadowsweet *(Spiraea latifolia)*, 59
Meal worms, 55
Mexican Double Yellow-Headed Parrot, 62-63, 109
Millet sprays, 54
Mites, 38-39
Mocking bird food, 53
Molting period:
  seeds for, 58
  treatment during, 41-43
Moon, E. L., 97
Morse, Richard, 57

INDEX

Mountain Ash *(Pyrus aucuparia)*, 59
Mouse Bloodwort *(Hieracium pilosella)*, 59
Mouse-Ear Chickweed *(Cerastium vulgatum)*, 59
Mouse-Ear Hawk's Beard *(Hieracium pilosella)*, 59
"My Experiences with Cockatiels," Moon, 97

Narrow-Leaved Plantain *(Plantago lanceolata)*, 60
National Exhibition, England, canary breeders, 3
Nervousness, 30
Nesting, 49-50
  material, 49
Nipplewort *(Lapsana communis)*, 60
Norwich Canaries, Their Breeding, Management, and Exhibiting, House, 97

Our Lady's Thumb *(Polygonum persicaria)*, 59
Out-of-door aviaries, 89-95
Overgrown bill, 37
Overgrown claws, 37

Page, C. N., 96
Palestine, 2
Panama Parrot, 63, 108
Parakeets, 4-5, 63-64, 104, 105
  feeding, 71-72
Parasites, 38-40
Parrot fever, 73-74
Parrots, 4, 107, 108, 109, 110
  best talkers, 62-63
  breeding, 68
  buying, 61-64
  care of, 65-70
  choosing, 62-64
  feeding, 66-68
  gentle and quieter, 63-64
  teaching to talk, 68-70
Parrots and Other Talking Birds, Page, 96
Parson Finch, 103
Pekin Nightingale, 4
Perches, 12
Plants, wild, 54-57-60
  thirty common, 58-60
Pneumonia, 28-29
Procedures, general, care of sick birds, 20-22
Prostrate Knotweed *(Polygonum aviculare)*, 59
Psittacosis, 73-74
Purchasing a bird, 6-10

Quassia water, 39
Queen of the Meadow *(Spiraea Catifolia)*, 59
Questions Answered About Cage Birds, Dick, 97

Rattails, 41, 58
Red-Headed Conure, 106
Red-Headed Gouldian Finch, 101
Red-Headed Parrot Finch, 101
Reproductive systems:
  cock, 75
  hen, 75-78
Respiratory system, 83-85
  ailments, 25-29
Revised Encyclopaedia of Cage Birds, Canaries, Parakeets, Mules and Hybrids, Fugg, 97
Ribbon Finch, 3
Ribwort *(Plantago lanceolata)*, 60
Richmond, Dr. C. W., 46
Roller Canary, 3, 26

INDEX

Roller Canary, *All About its Song and Training*, Gutierrez, 97
Rules for health, 17-18
Rye Grass *(Lolium perenne)*, 59

Saffron Finch, 3
Sandwort *(Spergula arvensis)*, 60
Scabrious Knapweed *(Centaurea scabiosa)*, 59
Scotch Fancy Canary, 100
Scurvy Grass *(Barbarea verna)*, 60
Seaweeds, 54
Septic fever, 29
Serin Finch, 1-3
Serinus serinus canarius, 1, 2
Sex of birds, telling, 44-45
Shaft-Tailed Finch, 3
Shama Thrush, 4
Shell Parakeets, 5, 63, 104
Shepherd's Purse *(Capsella bursa-pastoris)*, 60
Shock, 31-32
Silverbill, 3
Singing, 6-7, 51
Society Finches, 3, 11
Sore eyes, 32
Sore feet, 32-33
Speaking to bird, 7-8
Spice Finch, 3
Spray millet, 54
Star Thistle *(Centaurea nigra)*, 59
Stinking Willie *(Sebacio jacobaea)*, 60
Strawberry Finch, 3
Stroke, 31-32
Stuck in the molt, 42-43
Succory Dock *(Lapsana communis)*, 60
Superb Tanager, 103
Sweating, 30
Symptoms, common ailments, 22-35
Syrup of Buckthorn, 21
Syrup of Rhubarb, 21
Systema Naturae, Linnaeus, 1

Talking Budgerigars and How to Train Them, Wilson, 96
Tanagers, 4
Tansy or Tansy Ragwort *(Sebacio jacobaea)*, 60
Teaching the Budgerigar to Talk, Flowers, 96
Training, 96-98
Treatment, common ailments, 22-35
Troupial Bird, 4
Turquoise Green Parakeet, 105

Undulated Grass Parakeets, 5

Veterinarian, 19, 20, 29, 32, 34, 36, 74
Voice, loss, 26-27

Water-cress *(Nasturtium officinale)*, 60
Watmough, W., 97
Waxbills, 3
Weaverbirds, 4
Wetmore, Dr. Alexander, 46
Wheeziness, 26-27
White Campion *(Lychnis alba)*, 58
White Man's Foot *(Plantago major)*, 41, 42, 58, 60
White Parakeets, 64
White Yorkshire Canary, 99
Whydas, 4
Wild Canary, 1

INDEX

Wild Mustard *(Brassica arvensis)*, 58-59
Wild plants, 54, 57-60
   thirty common, 58-60
Wilson, Andrew, 96
Wing, fracture, 36
Winter Cress *(Barbarea vulgaris)*, 60
Worms, 40
Wounds, 36

Yellow Chopper Canary, 100
Yellow Dock *(Rumex crispus)*, 59
Yellow Parakeets, 64
Yellow Rocket *(Barbarea vulgaris)*, 60
Yellow-winged Sugarbird, 4
Young birds, 51-52

Zebra Finch, 3, 58

Printed in Great Britain
by Amazon